A COMPLETE GUIDE TO SPORTS AGENTS

A COMPLETE GUIDE TO SPORTS AGENTS

ROBERT O'CONNOR
Pierce College

WCB Wm. C. Brown Publishers

Cover photo by Bob Coyle
Cover design by Jeanne Marie Regan

Library of Congress Catalog Card Number: 89-85677

ISBN 0-697-10774-4

Printed in the United States of America by Wm. C. Brown Publishers, 2460 Kerper Boulevard, Dubuque, IA 52001

10 9 8 7 6 5 4 3 2 1

Contents

APPENDICES:

Preface

The objective of this book is to alert athletes, parents, coaches, athletic departments, agents, and legislatures about the advantages and problems of professional representation by agents and management groups.

The adverse publicity recently associated with some dishonest agents has brought into focus the need for more information to all concerned people. It has been so easy for the dishonest agents to overwhelm a number of top professional prospects with cash payments, even though such payments can cause many more problems than agents will admit. Because of dishonest actions of some agents and athletes, a university may be forced to forfeit games or championships, or be eliminated from bowl game consideration.

While dishonest agents abound and reap the majority of publicity, honest and competent agents do exist. A major focus of this book is to alert athletes as to how to find and employ such agents.

Another message of the book is to indicate to agents and potential agents the scope of services that can be offered as part of the agenting package. So many people think that negotiating a contract is the only function of an agent. And while it is important, it is only one of a number of functions that an agent should perform.

This book is the result of a great deal of research. Perhaps the most important element of that research was a nationwide survey of agents, athletes (both college seniors and professionals), athletic directors, coaches, the NCAA, and representatives of professional athletes associations. These surveys pinpointed the major needs that are addressed herein.

It is imperative that all concerned with the link between college athletics and professional sport be aware of both the problems and the potentials of the management of professional athletes. Athletes must protect themselves by choosing representatives who are honest and competent. Associations of professional athletes, as well as the NCAA and NAIA, have large stakes in making certain that the relations between athletes and agents is above board.

And perhaps the federal government must be brought into the picture to regulate the activities of agents.

I have attempted to develop the best thinking in every area of sports agenting but not every reader will be interested in every chapter of this book. Athletes, their parents, and advisors will be most interested in what they can expect agents to do and how to evaluate agents. Legislators may be most interested in the chapters on regulations and athletic department personnel will surely be interested in the total presentation.

Acknowledgments

I am very grateful for those who participated in the national survey. Most of the athletes, coaches, agents, and athletic directors responded anonymously, however, a few noted that their names could be used. Special thanks to coaches Joe Paterno and Larry Smith, and to agents Bob Woolf, Steve Arnold, Tony Attamasio, and F. Harrison "Buzz" Green.

Thanks also for the continued assistance of the administrators of the NCAA, the National Football League Players Association, the National Basketball Players Association, the Major League Baseball Players Association, the National Hockey League Players Association, the Canadian Football League Players Association, the Association of Representatives of Professional Athletes, and the state legislators who have been instrumental in passing laws regulating agents.

A very special thanks to Professor Lionel "Lon" Sobel of Loyola University Law School in Los Angeles. Professor Sobel is recognized as the leading legal mind attempting to set intelligent guidelines and legal regulations for sports agents.

ONE

Introduction

Why Should Athletes Have Agents?

Every person needs expert advice from time to time—we see our doctors, lawyers, and accountants when we are not experts in these fields of endeavor. The professional athlete is no different. With the complexity of contracts and the world of finances every professional athlete needs assistance. He or she is well advised to have a competent business advisor, attorney, tax expert, and friend.

A good agent allows the athlete to concentrate on performing and can also offer realistic advice on such things as: a player's true value to a team; how a player can enhance his or her value to a team through social service; what the player can plan for following his or her athletic career.

As most players know, a good agent can assist a player to get maximum value for his or her services, both as a player and as a product endorser. And the less sought-after free agents can often be placed with teams if they have competent and well-known agents.

According to Ed Garvey, former executive director of the National Football League Players Association, ". . . you need a negotiator. You need tax/financial advice, and you may need help with investments. As a rule of thumb, stay away from investments where your advisor has an interest."[1]

Who Are the Agents?

At the present time, anyone can be an agent for a player who has not yet signed with a team. Once the player has signed his first contract some players unions require that the agent be certified by the union in order to represent the athlete in future contractual negotiations.

The most commonly represented agents are lawyers. But accountants, businessmen, insurance salesmen, and former coaches are also widely represented. In actuality, all a person needs to become an agent is a client.

California law defines an agent as one who: (1) solicits an athlete to enter an agency contract or any professional team sports contract, or (2) for a fee, offers, promises, or attempts to help someone obtain a job with a professional sports team.

History of Commercialism in U.S. Athletics

Yale University first brought commercialism to college athletics when they hired a professional rowing coach to assist in the contest with Harvard. As football became the popular contest between colleges, many schools began paying both coaches and players to represent them—this practice started in the late 1800s.

While commercialism in athletics has been with us since the earliest days of college sport, the pay at the professional level only recently reached the point where it was worthwhile for business management to be involved. Red Grange utilized a representative in his negotiations with the Chicago Bears in 1925. He received the astronomical sum of $100,000 to play eight games in eleven days. However, it wasn't until the late 1960s that agents began to be seen in negotiation for top athletes. Earl Wilson with the Detroit Tigers and Jim Ringo with the Green Bay Packers are notable examples of athletes who sought representation during this time.

Earl Wilson, Tigers pitcher, tried a novel approach to negotiating his 1967 contract. At that time, having an agent with the player during negotiations was not allowed. So Wilson first met with an attorney and together they decided upon what to ask. On the day of the contract meeting Wilson went to the Detroit office by himself. However, every time he had a question about the progress of the negotiations he would leave the office and call his attorney.

Jim Ringo was the ten-year veteran center for the Green Bay Packers from 1953 to 1963. His negotiation tactics were not quite as productive. When he went to Vince Lombardi's office with an agent, he was promptly traded to Philadelphia.

Today most professional athletes have agents. Even though the number of college athletes needing agents is very small (only about one percent), that elite group has been subjected to many pressures to sign with agents. Recently there has been more and more publicity about dishonest agents signing players to contracts before their collegiate eligibility has been completed.

As the problems involving dishonest and incompetent agents have become more obvious, the legitimate agents, the colleges, the professional teams, and the state legislatures have become more vocal in setting standards for this highly important business activity.

Why Are Agents Needed?

No one can be an expert on everything. We seek the advice of medical doctors for our physical health, psychologists for our mental health, and accountants for our financial health. There is an old saying that "to be truly ignorant, one must be satisfied with his own opinions."

College athletes, as well as most other people in society, are not yet wise to the ways of the business world. Even the existing professional athletes are often taken in by "deals" that seem sensible. As our world becomes more complicated we need more expert advice on nearly every matter.

It is an unhappy fact that relatively few college athletes graduate from college (27 percent of Division I basketball players and 30 percent of Division I football players). Of those who make the professional teams, 33 percent of pro football players and 20 percent of pro basketball players have graduated from college. Those who have not graduated have little to fall back on when their professional careers end.

A professional career for a football player lasts 3.5 years and according to Dick Shultz,[2] executive director of the NCAA, half are divorced and bankrupt when their careers end. The average pro baseball career is four years; the average professional basketball player's career is five years. Given the high salaries of the NBA, it would be possible for a professional basketball player with competent management advice to have an adequate nest egg after five years.

Rules Governing Agents

The rules governing agents come from the NCAA, the colleges, and some players associations. Specific guidelines come from some state legislatures. And from every state, there are general legal guidelines on contract law, fiduciary responsibility, and fraud.

Honest and Competent Agents

Honest agents have guided their clients fairly and have not been driven to make a "quick buck" on them. They generally give competent representation of their clients in contract negotiations. They give sound financial advice. They work to get their most famous athlete's endorsement money for advertising products and services. And they seek the best interests of their clients.

Dishonest Agents

Dishonest agents' primary goal is to make money for themselves. They seduce clients to sign early by giving them illegal gifts, loans, or bonuses in an attempt to get a maximum professional contract for their clients—strictly for the agent percentage. They are not looking out for the best interests of their clients but instead are:

putting their clients in jeopardy of lawsuits for fraud from their colleges;

risking the university's forfeiting of games;

putting their clients at risk of civil and criminal lawsuits from the government if they fail to disclose the illegal payments on their tax returns.

The dishonest agents are most likely to put their clients' money into insurance programs or limited partnerships in which the agent gets a kickback, a sales commission, or a bonus. They attempt to get additional money, far beyond their commission fees, and therefore cheat the athlete even more.

Incompetent Agents

Both honest and dishonest agents may be incompetent. The agent may not know the value of a player to a team. Anthony Muñoz, of the Cincinnati Bengals, signed a contract which turned out to be well below what he was worth for his first several years. He later tried to get reimbursed in his next multiyear contract but was not successful. If an agent does not know the ropes in the initial negotiations, the athlete is likely to be underpaid—and there is no legal recourse for this situation.

Another area in which incompetence arises is in financial management. There are so many "deals" available to people with money. The problem is that many are either poor risks or outright frauds. Just ask Tony Dorsett or Kareem Abdul-Jabbar about poor financial management by their agents.

Summary

Most athletes need competent representation. The field of athletic agenting attracts many people—not all of whom are honest or competent. Athletes, with the help of their university athletic departments, should investigate the backgrounds and competencies of anyone whom they desire to have represent them.

Footnotes

1. Ed Garvey, *Selling Players Short* (Washington, D.C.: Federation of Professional Athletes AFL-CIO, 1984).
2. Dick Shultz, ''Integrity: The Key to Governance in College Athletics,'' address before the convention of the American Alliance for Health, Physical Education, Recreation, and Dance, April 9, 1988.

TWO

Agents and Negotiation

Most people think that agents just negotiate contracts and help athletes to maximize their bargaining potentials. And for many that is all that they do. However, many agents act as managers and many have teams of specialists to assist them in serving their clients.

The services that agents may perform are: negotiations, marketing the athlete to teams (primarily the lower draft choices and free agents), tax planning and preparation, insurance planning (health, life, disability), financial management, securing endorsements for their clients, providing psychological services, and directing their physical conditioning programs.

Marketing the Athlete to Employers

The pre-draft marketing for football can include sending resumés and films of the athlete to professional teams—the NFL, the Canadian League, European teams, and arena teams. The respected agents can also "push" their clients with the personnel directors of the teams.

Free agents who are not in the draft, such as those who have been cut or who have been out of football for a year or two, are often lost in the files of the teams. Agents can make the teams aware that their clients are ready to give pro football another try. Arena and spring football leagues and lower level professional basketball and baseball leagues are always options.

For those football players who fail to make a team in the United States or Canada there is the option of playing and/or coaching in foreign countries. With over a thousand American football teams in Europe, 600 in Japan, and 40 in Australia, there is a market for players who want to stay in the game as player coaches. Basketball players often can be placed with professional teams in other countries, especially in Europe. There is even professional water polo in Italy. Some agents have contacts to get players jobs in these areas.

The day after the draft, agents are in constant communication with teams to attempt to sign their free-agent clients. The more competent agents will try to interest teams in the athletes. Once they have interest from a team they will work to negotiate a contract. If several teams are interested they may look for the team that offers the best chance for success for the client.

Marketing the Playing Professional

For athletes who are playing in professional sports there is often the opportunity to market them as spokesmen for corporations for commercials or for speaking engagements. One of the most common types of endorsement is with shoe companies. When Walter Payton wore Kangaroo shoes he undoubtedly interested a great many players in buying those for themselves.

The athletes who are high profile (quarterbacks, running backs, and linebackers) in good media areas (New York, Chicago, or Los Angeles) can often make a great deal of money through endorsements. One rather noted quarterback was able to add over three million dollars a year to his one million dollars annual salary through endorsements.

Sometimes associating the athlete with other celebrities can increase his or her commercial value. Playing in celebrity golf or tennis tournaments or identifying with a charity can make the athlete more visible and more saleable to commercial interests.

Having the athlete give money back to his or her high school or college or working with a charity is good public relations for the player and team and is encouraged by some agents. Naturally the better the image of the player in the local and national community the greater the value of the athlete in the commercial realm.

Sometimes the name and appearance of the player can be used to gain a portion of a business the player's time and name traded for an interest in the business.

Negotiations

The **negotiations** can be handled by the agent, who may be a lawyer or accountant. Some of the more respected agents will have a lawyer, accountant, financial analyst, and another tax specialist on the negotiation team.

The place in which a player is drafted indicates, to a large degree, the maximum amount of money that player is worth. Quarterbacks may be paid a higher amount than the average; kickers and punters will generally be paid less than a field player would have been paid if selected in the same spot.

Of course, if the agent doesn't know the ropes, the player may well sign a contract for a lot less than he or she is worth. For example, a few years ago a player signed with a new agent for a discounted commission. The agent got this first-rounder a three-year contract for $167,000. Since the player was worth $500,000 a year, his agent cost him a million dollars over the three-year length of the contract.

Beginning agents will generally not know what other players in the league are being paid so when a general manager says "no players in that category are being paid that much" the agent may have no comeback. An experienced agent, on the other hand, should know the true value of a player.

Experienced agents also look at the strengths and weaknesses of the team to assess the bargaining power of the player. If a team gives away a high draft choice or trades away a strong player, it will strengthen the bargaining power of the athlete.

Another reason to have an agent represent the athlete is because the agent can drive for a hard bargain, and though this may irritate the club management, it is the agent, not the athlete, who draws the ire of the club. This protects the good relationships of the athlete with the team ownership and management.

Athletes at the low end of the scale, such as minor league baseball players, may not gain much from an agent. The athlete has no real bargaining power and the low-level salaries are already set. Some established pros have done their own negotiating and have kept their salaries relatively low on purpose. When the skills of two players are equal, or nearly equal, the club will probably keep the player with the lower salary. Louis Dampier, an NBA player, credited his tenure to his lower self-negotiated salary. He said other players who were equal or better were released while he was retained—just because of his lower salary. In the long run he made more money and had more fun.

Contract Structuring

The ***structuring of the contract*** is very important. Some of the less knowledgeable or less caring agents may take all of the money up front, then take their commissions and run. Other agents will extend the contract terms over a longer period of time so that the tax consequences are reduced. The player will then have more money extended over the coming years.

Various clauses can be added to the contract to protect the player. Often a player signs as a free agent or low-round draft choice then becomes a starter for the team, but has to play several years for the free-agent salary ($50,000 to $80,000) that was negotiated. The more knowledgeable agents insert clauses that protect the athlete in case his or her performance is greater than expected. They may also insert clauses to protect against other inflationary factors such as a new league forming. You may recall when the USFL lured NFL players with astronomical salaries. Those NFL players who were still under contract were stuck with lower salaries than their USFL counterparts.

An agent might even negotiate with a team that they will not sign another player at the same position as the player being represented. The team may not like the idea but it can still be discussed as part of the contract.

Few contracts are guaranteed. The so-called "no cut" contracts guarantee a player a salary even if he does not make the team. Very few contracts have this provision. Estimates are that under four percent of contracts are guaranteed.

With the exception of the "no cut" contracts a team can terminate an athlete at any time because of a "lack of skill." And it is the team that decides whether or not that skill exists.

Another ploy often used by a team is to have the player sign a series of one-year contracts. This limits the team's responsibility in case the player is injured. With a multiyear contract an injured player might have to be placed on *injured reserve* for years; with a one-year contract it need be only for the duration of that year. But injury guarantees can be put into the contracts—competent agents usually do this.

Tax Consequences

The *tax consequences* of the contract can be considerable. The more income the athlete can keep the better off he or she will be financially. Competent tax advisors can effectively maximize the amount of money retained through several avenues.

Another method of saving money is through the use of a personal services corporation that the management group can set up. With such a vehicle much of the athlete's extra income can be put into the corporation and many expenses, such as insurance, can be paid with pre-tax dollars.

The Signing Bonus

The *signing bonus* can vary from over a million dollars for a number one pick to nothing for a lower rated free agent. Most free agents will get signing bonuses in the neighborhood of $2,000 to $5,000. The amount of signing bonus, salary, and other financial aspects of a contract varies from team to team.

The Reporting Bonus

The *reporting bonus* is another possible element in the contract. Occasionally a player will take the signing bonus and run. This is rare, but it does happen. In order to guard against this occurrence teams may put part of the bonus money into a reporting bonus.

The Salary

The *salary* is a major concern of the player. The minimum salary for each sport for the 1988 season was:

Baseball	$ 68,000
Basketball	$100,000 (for first-year players)
Football:	
NFL	$ 50,000
Canadian League	$ 26,000
Hockey	$ 25,000

The average salaries are much higher. The average basketball player makes $515,000 and the average baseball player's salary is $512,000, with one in six making over a million dollars a year.

As was mentioned, the salary depends upon the need of the team for that player's talents and the financial ability or desire of the owner or manager to meet the player's demands.

Deferred Salary

Deferred salary is a method of extending the player's salary over more than one year. This allows the player to have income after retirement and also reduces the tax consequences in any one year. In deferring a salary the club acts as an insurance company offering an annuity policy. The player will get more total money by having the payments extended over a period of years.

As an example of how this works, Steve Young was offered two contracts when he became eligible for playing professional football. The Cincinnati Bengals offered him about $3.6 million; the Los Angeles Express, of the USFL, offered him $40 million over 43 years. He took the latter. Actually the two contracts were worth about the same amount of money—$3.6 million in an annuity would yield about $40 million over 43 years. Of course the USFL folded and the Express went bankrupt so Steve did not get much of the money. When he went back to the NFL he had to go as a second-string quarterback which was not the starting job he probably would have had with the Bengals.

Incentives

Incentives are negotiated by both the player's union and the player's agent. Some unions have negotiated awards to players who are named to all-league teams or who win special awards such as "Rookie of the Year."

Agents may negotiate such incentives as: the number of plays in which the player participates; making the starting team; scoring touchdowns; a quarterback's passing efficiency; or having the player meet a certain weight level.

Loans

Loans from the club for large purchases, such as a house, are also often possible. In some cases the contract may contain provisions for the loan to be forgiven after a certain time.

College Tuition

College tuition is often included in contracts for those who have not yet graduated or who are going for advanced degrees or additional education during the off-season.

Additional Benefits

Additional contract benefits for some players have been included in the total package. Kareem Abdul-Jabbar was allowed to use the Forum one day a year for his personal whim. Otis Birdsong's contract with the Cleveland Cavaliers included a clause that gave him 50 cents for each ticket sold over 5,000. Gus Williams' contract with Seattle included a white Rolls Royce.

Holding Out

Holding out a player is often counterproductive for the player. When first-round pick Kelly Stouffer was held out of the 1987 season, he lost a good deal of money and a chance to play for the year. Other players have lost a good deal of money and playing time in holding out. Todd Bell and David Duerson of the Chicago Bears held out the whole year the Bears went to the Super Bowl.

In 1988 Anthony Muñoz of the Cincinnati Bengals held out for more money. His agent, Howard Slusher, said that Anthony had been underpaid for his earlier years and that those good years should be paid for retroactively. The Bengals disagreed believing that if the athlete or the agent had not done an effective job of designing the contract originally, that was Anthony's problem. Muñoz finally agreed to a new contract, which was much closer to the Bengal's offer than to Slusher's demands.

Competent agents get their players the maximum amount of money, then get them into camp. A player is worth only so much money to a team. Often the owner does not place the same value on the athlete's services as the player does. So often discretion is the better part of valor and it is generally better for the player to play rather than hold out.

Another factor against holding out is that if the player is marketable for sponsorships or commercials, a holdout can reduce his value as a commercial property. Rather than holding out, a player who has become a free agent can use bargaining power to threaten leaving the team.

There are few opportunities for a holdout to sell his talents. Unlike a lawyer who may apply to hundreds of law firms, the athlete has few options. An NFL football player can play in Canada, a pro baseball player can play in Japan, and an NBA basketball player can play in a lower league or in Europe. But in most cases he is going to take a pay cut to do so. So holding out seldom works for the athlete.

Renegotiation

Renegotiation can be done at any time—unless a player has a contract clause that forbids it. Some players believe that they are more valuable than their salaries indicate and ask for a renegotiation of their contract salaries upward. For obvious reasons players who have poor years do not ask for a renegotiation to reduce their salaries.

Wayne Gretzky signed a multimillion-dollar contract for 21 years when he was 19 years old. Two years later it was agreed that he was worth much more so a new contract was negotiated.

In 1980 New England Patriots fullback, Sam "Bam" Cunningham asked for a renegotiation. Management refused so Sam sat out the year. The next year he got a much higher two-year contract. The question always is whether or not a player can make up the money lost when he holds out.

On the other hand, Seattle Supersonic center Jack Sikma refused to ask for a renegotiation even though his wages of $180,000 were very low for such a high-caliber player. Once he was able to renegotiate, he got $1.2 million per year for his next three years.

Generally, in order to get the club to renegotiate, the player must have some leverage, such as having had an outstanding year or perhaps unfairness or a lack of clarity in the original contract. Oral promises or unwritten expectations could also be reasons for renegotiating.

In football and basketball, where multiyear contracts are more common, the player is locked into a salary. It is quite possible that the player will be worth more before the contract runs out. In baseball, younger players are often given only one-year contracts. This requires them to wait only that one year before renegotiating a contract at the end of the year. Many agents believe that this is fairer than the multiyear contract.

To eliminate the problems of having to ask for renegotiation, the athlete and agent should insert a clause into the contract that allows for renegotiation if the player has a particularly good year. However, management might protect itself by not giving as high a salary the first year. Remember that in every contract there is give and take by both parties. If one party to the contract wants a special provision, the other party will probably ask for a provision to protect itself.

There should, of course, be no unwritten promises relating to the contract because they need not be honored—especially if the team is sold. This happened to Larry Bowa with the Phillies. The new management refused to honor the oral promises of the previous owner; the oral promises were not legally enforceable.

Some years ago Dwayne Thomas of the Cowboys claimed he was told that the Cowboys would tear up his contract if he had a successful year. Even though he was "Rookie of the Year" and the Cowboys went to the Super Bowl, Thomas was refused a new contract. The person who reportedly made the promise later said, "We say a lot of things to those young men to get them to sign."[1]

The Qualifications of the Negotiator

The competent negotiator should have a strong background in contract law and tax law, and extensive experience in negotiating. Negotiating experience in areas other than athletics gives a special expertise that can be brought to the negotiating table with professional teams. He should also be familiar with the specific problems and opportunities of negotiating with professional athletic teams.

Generally, the more experience a person has, the better he can advise the athlete about the desirable elements of the contract. The athlete can then choose what he wants in the finished document. Generally, both the team and the athlete must give and take; but, the experienced negotiator is better able to get what the athlete wants most.

Examples of Starting Contracts of the NFL

One can see from the following list of salaries from the 1986 first-round draft that one's place in the draft does not necessarily indicate the amount of signing bonus, the salary, or the total salary package. Because of the ability or the ineptitude of the negotiator and the financial generosity of the team, there are differences. By looking at the 1986 selections you can also get an idea as to whether the team or the player got the better deal. (See chart on next page.)

Such figures bring a few questions to mind. Are the Raiders more generous than the Rams? Why are Eric Dorsey (19th pick) and Tim Green (17th pick) making identical amounts? Why is Leslie O'Neal (8th pick) making more than the 4th, 5th, 6th, and 7th picks? Was it the agent's talent or the team's bottom line figure? Was it really worth it for Gerald Robinson to sign only a two-year contract if his signing bonus was about $100,000 less and he made $60,000 per year less than he would have with a four-year contract? Would it have been possible just to open negotiations after the second year of a four-year contract? Or did he just want to get out of the snow and play in the Sunbelt?

Other questions include such factors as these: Should running backs be paid more than offensive linemen because they do not generally last as long in the league? Should offensive linemen be paid more than running backs because they often play longer for a team? Should a team (such as Dallas) pay less if the player is injured and plays only two years of a four-year contract (as in the case of Mike Sherrard)? If management is taking such a chance should the players have the right to renegotiate if they play well? Or should management also have the right to renegotiate if the player does not play well or is injured?

Looking at a few numbers from the 1987 draft we can ask:

Was D. J. Dozier (14th pick by the Vikings) underpaid at salaries of $135,000 for the first year and $150,000 for the second and an option year? (*His signing bonus was $360,000 with a $300,000 loan to be forgiven if he played over 50 percent of the time.*)

Was John Clay (15th pick of the Raiders) overpaid with a $510,000 signing bonus and salaries of $150,00, $175,000, $290,000, and $375,000 for his four years? (*Compared to Dozier he did very well.*)

Did Tony Woods (18th pick by Seattle) do better with a three-year contract with salaries of $150,000, $250,000, and $300,000? (*However, his bonus of $350,000 was deferred until 1990, 1991, and 1992.*)

Why did Ron Bernstein (24th pick of the Chargers) make a great deal more than the 19th, 20th, 21st, 22nd, and 23rd picks? (It probably had something to do with his agent's expertise in negotiating.)

Name/Team	Pos.	Signing Bonus	Base	Years	Total Package
1. Bo Jackson/Buccaneers	RB	(signed pro baseball contract)			
2. Tony Casillas/Falcons	NT	$1,425,000	$175,000	4	$2,350,000
3. Jim Everett/Rams	QB	$1,200,000	$200,000	4	$2,550,000
4. Jon Hand/Indianapolis	DL	$ 775,000	$180,000	4	$1,745,000
5. Anthony Bell/Cardinals	LB	$ 650,000	$175,000	4	$1,580,000
6. Jim Dombrowski/Saints	OL	$ 600,000	$200,000	4	$1,575,000
7. Brian Jozwiak/Chiefs	OL	$ 600,000	$175,000	4	$1,475,000
8. Leslie O'Neal/Chargers	LB	$ 600,000	$200,000	4	$1,750,000
9. John Rienstra/Pittsburg	OL	$ 600,000	$175,000	5	$1,932,000
10. Keith Byars/Philadelphia	RB	$ 400,000	$200,000	4	$1,775,000
11. Joe Kelly/Cincinnati	LB	$ 625,000	$185,000	4	$1,555,000
12. Chuck Long/Lions	QB	$ 700,000	$200,000	4	$1,750,000
13. James FitzPatrick/Chargers	OL	$ 565,000	$165,000	5	$1,875,000
14. Gerald Robinson/Vikings	DL	$ 325,000	$100,000	2	$ 575,000
15. John L. Williams/Seattle	RB	$ 400,000	$157,000	4	$1,407,000
16. Ronnie Harmon/Buffalo	RB	$ 600,000	$150,000	4	$1,425,000
17. Tim Green/Atlanta	LB	$ 500,000	$150,000	4	$1,375,000
18. Mike Sherrard/Dallas	WR	$ 525,000	$155,000	4	$1,381,000
19. Eric Dorsey/Giants	DL	$ 500,000	$150,000	4	$1,375,000
20. Will Wolford/Buffalo	OL	$ 600,000	$150,000	4	$1,420,000
21. Tim McGee/Cincinnati	WR	$ 500,000	$150,000	4	$1,300,000
22. Mike Haight/Jets	OL	$ 300,000	$125,000	4	$1,250,000
23. Mike Schad/Rams	OL	$ 400,000	$125,000	4	$1,050,000
24. Bob Buczkowski/Raiders	DL	$ 500,000	$125,000	4	$1,200,000
25. Rod Jones/Buccaneers	DB	$ 500,000	$125,000	4	$1,145,000
26. Reggie Dupard/Patriots	RB	$ 400,000	$150,000	4	$1,300,000
27. Neal Anderson/Bears	RB	$ 425,000	$150,000	4	$1,300,000

Round-by-Round Differences in Football

Looking at the 1987 draft, there was a 10 percent increase in salary packages over the 1986 draft. The 1988 draft showed an additional 14 percent gain over 1987, but there had been a drop in salaries which occurred after the USFL expired.

The following is a compilation of the salaries given to those of the 329 draftees (1988 draft) who had signed by mid-August of 1988:

Round	Ave. Length	Ave. Yearly Contract	Ave. Signing Bonus	Ave. First Year Base
1	3.7 years	$480,000	$719,000	$199,000
2	3.6 years	$266,000	$240,000	$148,000
3	3.2 years	$192,000	$125,000	$111,000
4	2.9 years	$134,000	$ 70,000	$ 81,800
5	2.7 years	$117,000	$ 38,000	$ 74,000
6	2.4 years	$100,000	$ 23,000	$ 68,300
7	2.5 years	$ 94,500	$ 20,000	$ 66,700
8	2.5 years	$ 90,000	$ 16,000	$ 66,700
9	2.3 years	$ 87,300	$ 12,500	$ 64,700
10	2.3 years	$ 86,800	$ 10,700	$ 64,600
11	2.1 years	$ 82,700	$ 8,600	$ 63,000
12	2.2 years	$ 83,500	$ 7,400	$ 64,400

It is interesting to note that the average yearly contract and first-year base salaries were higher for the twelfth-rounders than for the eleventh-rounders. It can also be noted that while the top three rounds negotiated higher contracts than did the top three rounds in 1985, the lower rounds were lower than their 1985 counterparts. There is a great deal of "supply and demand" which must be taken into consideration in negotiating—and, as has been mentioned previously, the knowledge of the negotiator about professional athletics and the skill of the negotiator are of primary importance.

The 1988 draft salary packages showed that 45 of those selected did not do as well as those picked the year before in the same round. This has been attributed to players acting as their own agents or to those having inexperienced agents who did not know what the market was for the players. The following are a few specific situations that occurred:

A third-round quarterback who signed for seven percent more than the average second-rounder.

Two ninth-rounders who signed for deals better than the average sixth-round salary packages.

A twelfth-round quarterback with a salary equal to the eighth-round average.

There is also the continuing of the trend that quarterbacks are generally paid more while kickers and punters are paid less than other players selected in the same round. The so-called "skill" positions of runner, receiver, or defensive back were paid no more than were the linemen and linebackers. Another trend is that signing bonuses keep declining, especially below the second round. At the lower rounds (ninth through twelfth) the signing bonuses are 26 percent below the 1985 signees in the same rounds.

Free agents in 1988 received signing bonuses ranging from nothing to over $6,000. Their salaries generally were in the $55,000 to $65,000 range.

Summary

Anything can be negotiated in a contract. It can include everything from salary and a "no cut" clause to the jersey number. Both potential professionals and existing professionals should avail themselves of the finest talent available in negotiations. The athlete's agent should get as much money and as much security as possible for the player and the money gained should produce the most income for the player. It is therefore often advisable, for tax reasons, to take some of the salary deferred.

Footnote

1. Ed Garvey, *Selling Players Short* (Washington, D.C.: Federation of Professional Athletes AFL-CIO, 1984), p. 11.

THREE

Agents and Financial Dealings

A major mistake that many athletes make is assuming that the major job of the agent is to negotiate a contract. In reality the athlete should be thinking about beginning to establish lifetime financial independence.

A professional athlete has the opportunity of making a great deal of money in a short time. He should be thinking about his future. Too many newly rich athletes limit their thinking—their main concern is perhaps often contemporary, to buy a fancy car or move into a luxury apartment.

The highly paid athlete should remove as many of the financial worries from his or her mind as possible. If he or she has contracted with an honest and competent agent many worries can be reduced or eliminated.

Following are some of the services the more complete management groups may offer.

Financial Planning

Financial planning is an essential part of any athlete's overall business concern. With half of the NFL players bankrupt when they leave the league, there is an obvious need for competent financial planning.

A financial plan is like a game plan. It attempts to maximize strengths and potentials while minimizing weaknesses and risks. A sound financial plan will look at the present while preparing for the future. It should be sufficiently varied so that a problem in one area, such as one investment losing money, does not upset the whole plan.

A financial plan is unique to the individual. For example, a married player based in a high-rent area, such as New York or Los Angeles, will have different needs and expenses than a single player in Kansas City.

The tax consequences of a plan are also very important, however, they should not be thought of as the entire concern. Long-term goals should be the major concern in the plan.

The Financial Advisor

Finding a competent **financial advisor** is rather difficult in the agenting business. While nearly anyone may call himself a financial planner, the highest level experts in this field are called *Chartered Financial Analysts (C.F.A.)*. This appellation is a very difficult certification to achieve. It takes years of study and the passing of some very difficult examinations. Some agents are certified financial planners (CFP)—a very low level of certification, comparable to insurance salesmen.

Less-competent agents either do not concern themselves with expert financial planning or do not provide proper advice, which can, of course, result in major problems for the athlete. But so often the athlete or the agent is quite content with his own ineptitude because he does not know what is involved in effective and informed financial planning.

With effective financial planning even an athlete at a free agent's salary should have amassed $200,000 to $250,000 after four years. But if the salary has been "blown" on a Porsche, a Rolex, and an expensive rented apartment, the chances are there will not be much left for safe investments such as real estate or tax-free municipal bonds.

Investment Analysis

Analyzing potential investments is another possible service an agent may perform. Just as insurance companies and banks have their possible investments analyzed according to certain criteria, the athlete should also have his or her investments analyzed by experts. Celebrities are offered many financial opportunities—many of which are either unsound or outright scams. Even the most astute business people use other experts for their investment analyses. The lack of such expertise has led to the financial downfall of a great many professional athletes, among them Tony Dorsett and Kareem Abdul-Jabbar.

Portfolio Management

Portfolio management assists the athlete in choosing the better investments and in keeping the financial assets in the most productive vehicles such as real estate, stocks, bonds, treasury securities, or precious metals. The financial manager should assist the athlete in choosing the direction that the portfolio should take.

Conservative investments have a low chance of loss. Although the chance for high gains is rather low, it is most likely that the athlete will not lose money. Tax-free municipal bonds, real estate, and money market instruments, such as T-bills, are among the conservative investments.

Aggressive portfolios are more likely to include stocks, bonds, and limited partnerships. These investments have a greater upside but also a greater downside.

Any investment can gain or lose money. Real estate, which has generally been considered conservative, has increased at approximately 20 percent per year in parts of California but has lost considerable value in parts of Texas. No one knows for certain which investments will be most effective but an investor will have a far better chance of making money if the investment advisor is highly qualified and informed.

Some agents actively manage the portfolios under a power of attorney. Others simply advise the athlete of what should probably be done, then let the athlete make the final decision. This "hands-off" approach is generally recommended as the best way for the athlete to be in control. Most financial problems experienced by athletes have occurred when the agents handled all of the money.

Preferred Banking Status

Preferred banking status is a service that at least one management group has arranged for the athletes. Such a status is important in order to establish immediate financial ties to supply low interest rates when needed for such things as real estate and business loans.

Pension Plans

Some agents assist the athletes to incorporate themselves just as other professionals may do. The incorporation allows many tax benefits, including the purchase, in pre-tax dollars, of Keogh plans, Individual Retirement Accounts (IRAs), and tax-sheltered annuities. Such plans have to be approved by the Internal Revenue Service. The advantage of purchasing in "pre-tax" dollars is that the incorporated person can make some payments from the gross salary and then pay taxes on what is left.

The **pension plans** should be coordinated with other pensions and with social security. This type of planning takes expert accounting assistance. Considerations the tax and pension advisor might evaluate are:

Individual Retirement Account (IRA), which allows an employee or a self-employed person to contribute up to $2,000 per year in pre-tax dollars toward a retirement account.

Keogh plan, which allows an employee to contribute up to 15 percent of self-employment income up to a yearly maximum of $15,000. Income from interest and dividends is not included in "self-employment" income.

401 (K), which is a type of deferred income compensation plan that allows up to $7,000, or 25 percent, of income to be invested by the employer, with the proceeds paid out after retirement.

Tax-free municipal bonds, which allow a person to invest in bonds, with the interest on the bonds nontaxable. A broker can buy bonds which mature at times that will repay the investor at any time prior to or after retirement.

Insurance

Among the types of **insurance** an athlete may want are: medical, life, disability, and annuity plans. If the athlete is married these become of greater concern.

Some sports agents are insurance agents who sell the athlete insurance, then reap the commissions. Single-pay life insurance can carry commissions of 60 percent—what the athlete thinks is a small commission fee can become a huge fee if the agent sells insurance or takes kickbacks.

The more reputable agents will seek out the best deals for their players. Some of the larger management groups will bargain directly with the companies on behalf of several of their athletes seeking similar types of insurance coverage. The reputable agents consider their insurance negotiations as part of the job for which the athlete is paying a commission and therefore do not sell insurance or take kickbacks.

Tax Services

Since professional athletes make quite a bit of money they must pay taxes. **Tax services** actually start with the way the contract is negotiated, so as to reduce or delay taxation on the earnings.

Some agents have resident accountants who handle the taxes. Some agents just "arrange" for the tax returns to be done and then bill the athlete. Most of the reputable management groups include their tax services and handling the tax returns as part of their services for the one commission fee.

Top athletes who make endorsements, commercials, movies, and speaking engagements can invest a good deal of money in personal corporations, allowing the athlete to save money and pay many bills in pre-tax dollars. It also allows for additional retirement contributions that can also be made in pre-tax dollars.

Bill Paying and Bookkeeping

Some athletes have their entire checks sent to their agents or to their accountants. Their bills are paid by the accountant so tax deductions are easier to determine. Athletes are then sent an "allowance" they must budget themselves. The rest of their money goes into investments and savings accounts as they direct.

Having an accountant handle the bills reduces the time demands on the athletes and allows them to concentrate on performing. It also forces them to stay on the budget the financial analyst has developed. In addition, all of the tax records are at the accountant's office so the athlete does not have to deal with them at tax time.

Endorsement Money

Some professional athletes are worth a great deal as endorsers of products. Jim McMahon selling tacos or Gary Carter selling soap can make a great deal more money than their salaries.

Obviously some athletes are worth more money than others. The Super Bowl quarterback is worth more than the kicker on the last-placed team.

The following is what a few athletes made on endorsements during the 1987 year:

Boris Becker, 1986 Wimbleton champion	$5,000,000
Michael Jordan, basketball pro	$4,000,000
Greg Norman, golf pro	$4,000,000
Jim McMahon, quarterback	$3,000,000
Dennis Connen, sailer	$1,800,000
Gary Carter, baseball catcher	$ 700,000

If the endorsement money is handled through a personal services corporation there are often tax advantages that the agent and the tax advisors should be able to design to use to pay many of the athlete's expenses in pre-tax dollars.

Summary

Some agents only negotiate a contract. Some offer total services that can increase the net worth of the athlete and protect him or her from financial problems. The commissions they charge may or may not be a bargain. The agent's value depends upon how well the personal and financial concerns of the athlete are handled.

FOUR

The Agent's Role in Assisting the Athlete in Making Life Adjustments

There are agents who just want to negotiate a contract and then take the money and run. There are agents who do a fine job of representing their players. And there are agents who are friends of their clients and who want to see them successful in all walks of their lives.

Most players need advice and assistance in getting ready for their first pro camp. Some agents help them do this. Many players will need help during and after their careers in personal, financial, and vocational areas. Some agents enjoy offering such assistance.

Getting the Player Ready for Camp

Some agents hire strength and conditioning coaches to help their clients get bigger, stronger, and faster. Some will just monitor the progress of the player as he continues to use his college's weight training facilities. Some will bring the player to the agent's headquarters, pay his way, and supervise his conditioning. Of course this costs the player money and requires that the player drop out of school.

While agents may provide advice on workouts for strength, speed, and muscle hypertrophy, it is usually wiser for the athletes to stay at their home campus under the guidance of the college strength coach. These coaches are the best prepared experts in the country, have outstanding facilities, and the athletes can continue in school to complete their degree requirements.

Many players have to be focused on how important the preseason camp will be. Most players can't believe that there is a chance they won't make the squad. After all, they were outstanding in high school and college and have had dreams of glory days with the pros. The reality is that all of the other players in camp have also been outstanding athletes. And the returning pros have had experience which sets them ahead of the rookies. Further, the returning players look at a rookie as one who wants to take his $200,000-a-year job. And he doesn't like that thought a bit. So in order to make a professional team, a rookie must be primed to try harder, learn faster, and play better than ever before. A competent agent can help a great deal in this regard.

Completing College

Most athletes have not finished their college majors when they become professionals. The college degree is a "union card" for many good jobs which the player may desire after he finishes his playing career.

Some agents advise their clients to quit college when their eligibility is finished. They may take the athlete to their facilities and supervise his workouts. And, of course, the athlete gets billed for this "service." Athletes would be better served staying in school, completing their studies, and working with the better weight training equipment and the more competent coaches at the college.

While a college degree may not be essential to be a beer distributor, it is an essential for many jobs in business or in coaching. For these reasons the agent and athlete should work together to set a firm base for satisfying work and economic achievement after the professional playing days are over.

It is difficult to realize that most of one's working years will not be on the gridiron—but in an office. For this reason it is very important to finish college. As has been previously mentioned, college tuition for the athlete can be included in the contract. The tuition clause in a contract is often called the "mama clause" because mothers appreciate it so much.

Assisting with Personal Problems

Professional athletes may have greater personal problems than do the average citizens: the pressure to make the team; the weekly pressure to win; the continual references in the media. Such pressures may confuse and depress athletes, requiring them to seek psychological counseling.

The stress on the player can also cause stress in a marriage. Half of the players who leave the league are divorced when they leave. Marriage counseling is often in order. Concerned agents may assist their clients with these psychological problems by getting them effective therapists.

Other problems are not as psychologically severe. A player may want to buy or lease a new car, purchase real estate, or take out a loan. The agent can assist with these needs. Some include these services in their basic fees; some charge extra.

Alcohol and Drug Abuse

Most people either have some problems they would like to forget and/or they have a need to feel better. Alcohol, sleeping pills, and tranquilizers can make people forget about their troubles. Cocaine or amphetamines can give an orgasmiclike "high." But these mind-altering substances create more problems than they solve.

Many athletes adhere to the "All-American" ideal of living clean in mind and body. They feel good about themselves and get their highs from their performance on the field. Others cannot handle the pressure to perform, or they want to forget the harshness of the practice field by downing a beer or dropping a pill. One former Heisman Trophy winner had more than a few problems with drugs and was temporarily suspended from his starting job with the Rams. Stanley Wilson was dropped from the Bengal squad just prior to the 1989 Super Bowl because of his cocaine use the week prior to the game.

Today there is better education about substance abuse, more testing opportunities, and more effective treatment methods. Both the athlete and the agent should be alert to the overuse of alcohol and illegal drugs.

The professional leagues are now adopting harsher penalties for drug users and abusers. A suspension for drug use is not only costly, in terms of salary lost while suspended, but it is also very embarrassing for the player.

Preparing for Life after Athletics

Athletes face the same kinds of problems that others do: unemployment, underemployment, drug use, alcoholism, legal problems, injury, illness, marital and family problems. However, a major difference between the successful athlete and the average person is that the athlete has been in the limelight throughout high school, college years, and as a professional athlete. And as a pro athlete probably makes a great deal more money per year than he will after he "retires." The average person, on the other hand, usually works upward financially with a more gradual increase in salary each year, and "levels out" by retirement age.

The experienced agent should be willing to work with the athlete as a friend. The agent's own life experiences should be a guide to helping the athlete see the problems and potentials of the future. The agent who is not a friend will hurt the athlete more than he will help him. Many agents are interested only in the "quick buck," not in the athlete as a person.

The wise athlete will choose an agent who will assist him or her in developing and working on long-term goals. The player who forgets that the playing days will someday stop is in for some real personal and economic problems.

Summary

As life becomes more complicated many people require expert guidance in handling their lives, whether it be in the financial, the personal, or the social areas. Professional athletes, because of the nature of their employment, are subjected to more than the normal complement of stresses. The athlete should be concerned that the agent chosen is readily available whenever expert help is sought. This is where the athlete needs a friend, not just a financial advisor.

FIVE

Dishonest or Incompetent Agents

In 1986 agent Joe Courrege was sued by four professional football players—Jeff Rohrer and Bill Bates of the Dallas Cowboys, Anthony Dickerson of the Buffalo Bills, and Steve Wilson of the Denver Broncos. They noted that while he had enticed them into signing by spouting Christian principles, he had defrauded them with bogus corporations and fictitious names, and by putting them into several shady real estate transactions.

While the legitimate and honest agents continue to do their jobs effectively, the dishonest and incompetent agents keep gathering the publicity. This, obviously, leaves a very negative effect on the profession.

Dishonest acts by agents are centered primarily around: paying the athlete for early signing; paying an athlete to sign even when it is legal to sign (after the eligibility is completed and before the draft); making loans to college athletes, putting the athlete into insurance deals that are not giving top value for the money (with high commissions being paid to the agent); padding expenses charged to the athlete; and defrauding the athlete through crooked financial deals and embezzlement. Incompetence is found in poor negotiating, putting the athlete into poor business deals, or not getting the athlete the best insurance or financial advice available.

One of the major reasons for the problem is that there are no requirements, other than having a client, to become an agent. Because of this, recruitment of athletes is the major factor in becoming an agent. But the ability to recruit has nothing to do with competence or honesty.

How Competent and Honest Are the Agents?

In the survey of reputable agents, their estimates of dishonest agents varied from the observation of "quite a few" to percentages in the 25 to 30 percent range. Bob Woolf, one of the pioneers in the agenting business, has stated that he thinks about 25 percent of agents are dishonest. Ralph Cindrich believes that while about 10 percent break the law, probably 40 to 50 percent break the NCAA rules or the rules of the individual colleges.

F. Harrision "Buzz" Green, president of Pro Sports Management, thinks that of the 800 agents, about 30 percent are dishonest, 60 percent are honest but not competent to give effective representation, and about 10 percent are both honest and competent.

University of Southern California football coach Larry Smith has stated he believes that 50 percent of agents are unscrupulous. He and other coaches relate that many agents promise much more than they can deliver.

Any of these percentages are far too high for such an important and visible profession. The fact that a very high number of players are being poorly represented and/or cheated is certainly a cause for concern among intelligent professional athletes.

Who Are the Dishonest Agents?

Generally speaking, the agents who have had the most complaints against them are those in business promotion, insurance, theatrical agents and promoters, and people who have had ties with professional or college football.

The fewest complaints have been received on lawyers and CPAs. This is probably because they have too much to lose in terms of their licensing to risk dishonesty.

According to Fred Milverstedt, "Critics characterize the unethical agents as frustrated hustlers who have been unsuccessful in previous business ventures, and who find loopholes in existing regulations, or circumvent them completely, in order to prey on the young and naive."[1]

Signing Athletes Early

Perhaps the most flagrant violation of law and ethics is the **early signing** of athletes and the paying or loaning of money to them for the early signing. Such signing forces the athlete to violate the contract he has with the university, violates NCAA rules, and, if not reported as income, becomes a federal criminal offense.

The often indicted agent Norby Walters said that he usually approached the poor black athletes—especially those with single parents. It might be concluded that he could appeal to them on either a greed level or on a charitable level—telling them that they could help their families with the money. The middle-class black and white athletes are generally less likely to place their futures in jeopardy.

Because a great deal of money can be made by charging high fees and expenses, it is worth the risk for the dishonest agents to "make loans" to athletes who sign early. Many of these fast-talking charlatans lead the players to believe there is no danger in getting caught. And, in fact, most do not get caught by enforcement agencies. But they do "get caught in the web" of the dishonest agent and pay a high price financially for their folly. They end up with much less money than they would have if they had waited for honest representation. The fees they paid would have been lower, their salary negotiations would have been more effective, and their investments would have been handled more effectively.

Aundray Bruce, the number one pick in the 1988 football draft, said that agents had come to him with "actual shopping bags full of money" but that he decided to get his money the honest way. He said, "You just have to sit down and say, 'Hey, if I have patience, I'll receive mine the right way.' "

Some agents loan money then give the athlete an "offer sheet" in which the agent spells out what he will do for the athlete. After the athlete signs it, and the agent says it is not a binding contract until he signs it, which he won't until the season is over, the agent states this is legal and there is no violation of NCAA rules. This is not true—it is a violation of NCAA rules and it is also a contract.

What Is the Percentage of Illegal Early Contracts?

The noted West Coast agent, Leigh Steinberg, estimates that about 20 percent of the potential professional football players have illegal contracts. Jim Abernethy, a convicted former agent, estimates 80 percent have signed illegal premature contracts. He said that of the 200 to 250 players he talked to, all were either willing to take money or were already taking it from another agent. Jim Solano, a long-time agent, says that Abernethy might be right, that during his 18 years as an agent it has always been substantially more than half of the players who have signed early. While Solano deals mostly with NFL veterans, college players often seek him out and often ask him for money. But Ralph Cindrich, another long-time agent, thinks that the 80 percent figure is much too high.[2] F. Harrison "Buzz" Green, an agent for over 15 years, says that he has heard estimates of 30 to 60 percent and believes the higher figure to be closer to the truth.

Illegal Signing Bonuses or Loans

It is a violation of civil law as well as a breach of professional ethics to offer a player money to sign a contract. This is true even if the player's eligibility is completed.

This is illegal because in contract law the contract should give mutual benefit. If a player signs for a five percent fee the agent should be adequately paid and the athlete should be getting his money's worth. If the agent promises to give or lend money to the athlete in exchange for signing, it is a bribe and the athlete does not have to pay it back. Actually the agent will make certain that he gets all of his money back, and more, if the athlete stays with him.

One agent anonymously noted that he had given $10,000 and $15,000 early payouts to two athletes to sign in 1986. Others that he bribed stayed with him but these two did not and he had no legal recourse to getting his money back since it was illegally given and could be considered a gift. In 1987 he decided to give no more bribe money to early signers and he got no players for that year. Yet his expenses included the operation of his office, the expenses of his assistant who went to the Shrine Game in San Francisco, and for himself at the Hula Bowl. He decided that if he was going to remain in the agenting business he would have to start the illegal payoffs again. In June of 1988 he had already signed early contracts and given bribe money to several players.

Former agent Mike Trope has admitted that he lent money to college players.[3] He felt that it was alright because it was not a violation of law—only of NCAA rules.

In 1988 several University of Miami football players told school officials that agent Mel Levine had offered them $20,000 and the use of a car if they would sign with him. Levine denied the allegations.

In December of 1989 attorney and agent Ray Newman of Los Angeles sued several NFL rookies to recover money he had lent them while they were in college. The attorney alleges that Derrick Thomas (University of Alabama, Kansas City Chiefs) owes him $35,160; Deion Sanders (Florida State University, Atlanta Falcons) owes $28,460; Eric Hill (Louisiana State University, Phoenix Cardinals) owes $26,462; Broderick Thomas (University of Nebraska, Tampa Bay Buccaneers) owes $17,067; and Hart Lee Dykes (Oklahoma State, New England Patriots) owes $7,900. The attorney has stated that he never had a contract with the players or an agreement to represent them, he merely loaned them money when they needed it.

According to the NCAA's Bylaw 12 on amateurism (see Appendix B-1, 12.1.2), such loans make the athlete a professional who is ineligible to continue to participate on the university's team. The NCAA could, but probably would not, force the university to forfeit games. The university could sue for the return of the scholarship money. The athlete could also be sued for fraud against the university. The Internal Revenue Service could become involved because the scholarship money, which was tax deductible, would become taxable once the loan was accepted.

In late December, 1989, Johnny Rodgers, former Heisman Trophy winner, and the company he represented, Total Economic Athlete Management of America, Inc., were each fined $10,000 under the Texas law which forbids contact with athletes who still have college eligibility. It was alleged that Rodgers had met with the 1989 Heisman Trophy winner, junior Andre Ware, and had offered him $20 million to sign a professional contract. It was also found that Rodgers had bought Ware's mother a fur coat and other items. Rodgers denied many of the charges.

The author's survey of pro football rookies in 1988 indicated that two or three agents had offered them money. This number held true for the athlete who had been contacted the least (six times) and for the one who had been contacted the most (40 times).

Incompetence

Some agents may be well meaning but just do not "know the ropes." It takes a good deal of experience to understand the meaning of the collective bargaining agreements between the management and the unions. It takes knowledge of: the teams' negotiating postures, the importance of his client to the team, and contract structuring. These are not everyday bits of knowledge that some family friend knows. It takes a truly experienced professional. Just look at the signing bonuses and the salaries paid to the top draft choices and you will note that often the lower draft choices come out financially better than the higher ones because they had knowledgeable and competent negotiators.

Conflicts of Interest

There may often be a **conflict of interest** with an agent. He may be representing two or three people playing the same position for the same team. How will he handle this? He may be an insurance broker or a stock broker. If he sells his clients insurance this may be a conflict of interest. While lawyers are bound by their code of ethics to tell a potential client about such conflicts of interest, other agents may not be held to the same standard of ethics.

Another example of a conflict of interest is in golf or tennis. A player might be better off remaining an amateur for another year or more. But if the agent can get the player to turn professional he will gain a client. If the player remains an amateur for another year he or she might well choose another agent.

Mismanagement of Funds

Handling investments requires true expertise. Even the experts make some huge mistakes. The less expert are much more likely to be taken in by "get rich quick" schemes.

Since professional athletes often make great sums of money there is always the possibility that an athlete or agent will be taken in by dishonest business persons. Generally, the lower the return on an investment the greater its security. U.S. government bonds or bank accounts are very safe but have relatively low yields. Over-the-counter stocks and some limited partnerships may have great potential for gain but also may have great potential for loss. The incompetent agents, not understanding the true nature of the investments, may be taken in by false promises.

Dishonest agents have embezzled their athletes' funds or gambled them away and some have simply taken the money and left.

Excessive Fees

Today the fees are often regulated by the player associations. This protects the athletes. But, as in the case of rookie football players, they are not covered by the collective bargaining agreement so they can be charged excessive amounts.

One of the most common ploys of dishonest agents is to take all of their commission from the signing bonus of the player. If the player is cut the player ends up with a relatively small percentage of his bonus and salary. For example, if a player signed for a $200,000 bonus plus $100,000 a year for three years and was paying a 10 percent commission to the agent, he would pay a total of $50,000 over the three years. But if the agent took the $50,000 from the signing bonus and the player did not make the team, the actual commission would be 25 percent ($50,000 of the $200,000 signing bonus).

Criminal Complaints Against Agents

Of the agents working unethically or illegally only a small number get caught and those caught receive relatively small sentences or fines. This makes it a good risk for many who are interested in the "quick buck."

The problem with dishonest sports agents exploded in 1987 when World Sports and Entertainment run by theatrical agent Norby Walters and his associate Lloyd Bloom were exposed as having signed and paid a great many underclassmen. (More than 60 athletes were subpoenaed. Forty-three of these athletes have agreed to pay back their colleges for their scholarships in order to avoid prosecution.)

Running back Paul Palmer of the Kansas City Chiefs was one of those who admitted that during his senior year at Temple he accepted monthly payments and a $5,000 loan from Bloom and Walters in order to sign a contract early. He says that he has paid back all of the money.[4]

The prosecution of the 1989 case against Walters and Bloom revolved around fraud and racketeering. The fraud charges centered around the damage done to several universities because players had signed early contracts and had thus become ineligible to compete under NCAA rules. Players who compete ineligibly force the school to forfeit games. This in turn eliminates the schools from postseason competition with potential losses of millions of dollars in gate receipts and television money. (It is this money from football and basketball that funds the other sports for both men and women. Consequently the universities must drop nonrevenue-producing sports for both men and women when their income is reduced due to forfeiture of games in the revenue-producing sports.)

The racketeering charges were entered because Walters and Bloom allegedly used organized crime figures to enforce their contracts when sports or entertainment figures attempted to end their relationships with Walters and Bloom. Maurice Douglass, of the Chicago Bears, testified that Bloom threatened to "have somebody break my legs" if he stopped doing business with him without returning the money and the cars given him by Bloom and Walters. Everett Gay of the Detroit Lions offered similar testimony. One agent, who asked to remain anonymous, reported that there had been a contract on his life because he had disclosed the activities of Walters and Bloom. In another instance, Kathe Clements, an employee of agent Steve Zucker, was viciously beaten for allegedly signing athletes who had at one time been under contract to Walters and Bloom.

While the actual trial in the United States District Court in Chicago centered on defrauding certain universities, there were a number of other possible crimes the grand jury investigated and which might have been charged. Among the other possible charges were: mail fraud, wire fraud, failure of student athletes to report income, drug dealing, and prostitution.

The defense for Walters and Bloom maintained that the two agents had not broken any laws, only NCAA rules, and they further maintained that it was the athletes, not themselves, who had committed crimes or indiscretions. They pleaded not guilty to the charges of racketeering, mail fraud, wire fraud, and extortion. The government, however, maintained that the primary issue was fraud against the universities. On April 13, 1989 Walters and

Bloom were convicted by a jury that deliberated for 40 hours over a six-day period. The potential penalties for their actions were up to 55 years in prison and fines of up to $1.25 million. Their actual sentences consisted of five years in prison for Walters and three years for Bloom. Bloom was also ordered to repay $145,000 to Paul Palmer (money that Palmer had given him to invest) and fined $250,000. They plan to appeal the verdict.

U.S. Attorney Anton Valukas said that there is a message in the verdict: ". . . the message is that the federal criminal laws apply across the board to the universities, to the athletes, and the agents who do business with them." The results of this action may have a lot to do with how agents perform in the future. Federal Judge George Marovich also expressed the hope that the sentencing would bring the "rule of law" to big-time college sports.

In another action Bloom and Walters were sued by the University of Alabama to recover the $250,000 which the university had to return to the NCAA because it was denied participation in the NCAA postseason basketball tournament. The university sued for $3 million. Bloom was fined $2,000 and had to serve one week of a one-year sentence. His sentence was reduced because he agreed to testify against Walters. The settlement of the civil and penal cases against Walters were reportedly settled for $200,000, with an agreement not to conceal any dealings with eligible student athletes in the Southeastern Conference.

Other areas being investigated by various law enforcement agencies include possible point fixing by athletes, and possible collusion of some coaches with unethical agents—in exchange for money, some coaches direct athletes to agents.[5] At this time the NCAA does not have any knowledge of such actions by coaches, but notes that it is contrary to NCAA rules for a coach to act as an agent or to serve as a broker.

Jim Abernethy, who gave up being an agent in 1987 after being convicted of illegally signing and paying nine athletes prematurely, was convicted of a misdemeanor tampering charge and was sentenced to a year in jail and fined $2,000 for "tampering." The same jury found him innocent of bribery and of violation of "deceptive trade" law. These charges stemmed from his dealings with Auburn football player Kevin Porter.

When the charges against Abernethy were first leveled, he gave copies of the signed contracts to *The Atlanta Journal-Constitution.* The immediate result was that three players were declared ineligible for bowl games. He said that he knew his revelations would hurt the players but added, "These guys all knew what they were doing—every one of them. I mean, they'd sit there and bid and dicker with me."

He said he signed most of them to contracts during the summer prior to their senior year. He gave them a cash bonus to sign and $300 to $1,000 per month. He also gave them bonuses for playing well, such as when they scored touchdowns or made interceptions. He estimated that he spent $15,000 to $20,000 per player.

David Lueddekke, of California, pleaded guilty to federal charges of obstruction of justice and perjury as the result of a grand jury investigation in Chicago in 1988. He had engaged in illegal dealings with college athletes before their eligibility was completed. One of the players who received money was the Ohio State starting tailback and team captain Vince Workman. Workman testified that he had received $1,000 from Lueddekke in February of 1987. Because Workman had taken the money in violation of NCAA and university rules, he was declared ineligible for his senior year in 1988. On April 28, 1989 Lueddekke was fined $10,000 and given 26 months in prison. His penalties could have been as much as 10 years in prison and $500,000 in fines.

Former NBA player Dennis Duval lost $30,000 to his agent, Richard Sorkin. Duval then had to go through bankruptcy proceedings. Sorkin lost a total of about $1.2 million of his clients' money. He was sentenced to three years in prison.

What Athletes Can Do When They Believe They Are Cheated

When agents give money to an athlete to sign a contract with him it is a breach of civil law. The athlete can quite possibly get out of the illegal contract but, of course, there may be some problems because the athlete is not considered to have come into the action with what is legally called "clean hands."

Jerry Rice of the 49ers has sued his agent, Everett Glenn, for mismanagement. Eric Dickerson has sued former business agent Jack Rodri and the Ken Norton Management Agency for $12.5 million for financial mismanagement. Ken Norton has also sued Rodri. These are not the first athletes to sue an agent.

Former Ohio State Buckeye star Chris Carter has sued Norby Walters and Lloyd Bloom for $4 million alleging that the agents' dealings cost him his senior year of eligibility which reduced his place in the NFL draft. He believed that if he had played his senior year he would have gone higher in the draft than his fourth-round spot. This cost him a great deal of money. He also has said that the agents threatened him with physical harm if he did not live up to his agreement.

Kareem Abdul-Jabbar has sued former business manager Tom Collins to recover damages that he alleges to be $59 million. Abdul-Jabbar contends that Collins breached his fiduciary duty when he did not fully explain the risks of some of the deals. Collins has countersued Abdul-Jabbar for $382,000 in commissions and fees.

There may also be criminal law violations. All states have laws concerning fraud, embezzlement, and larceny. When an agent gives advice on investments he may come under the provisions of the Investment Advisers Act of 1940.[6] If he is not qualified to give investment advice he may be held liable for giving poor information.

The Effect on Honest Agents

As dishonest agents sign more players, the honest agents are left out in the cold. Their honesty has cost them valuable clients.

Ed Garvey, former executive director of the National Football League Players Association, has said that because the dishonest agents have contracted with so many players prior to being eligible to sign a contract, the players have cheated themselves. "You eliminate the best (player representatives) right away, and what you have left are a bunch of unsuccessful ones who believe all they need is one or two big names a year in order to make a couple hundred grand. If you allow this to continue you naturally select out the most talented people and leave the athletes, for the most part, to choose from a group of ne'er-do-wells."[7]

Looking to the Future

As dishonest agents are looking for easier and easier prey, the age at which they sign illegal contracts drops. So while illegal contracts are usually signed before the senior college season they are now being signed in earlier years—and we wonder if high school players may not be next.

One question is how can the illegal recruitment be stopped? It has been suggested that a type of "sting" operation could be possible with an athlete identifying an agent as having offered him money. The athlete might then be rewarded with the same amount of money. It wouldn't take many such operations to shut down most of the illegal signings.

Another ploy could be to give the athletes who have signed illegal contracts the legal aid to get out of the contract. Since the contract was illegal under civil law (because money was given in addition to the terms that a fair contract requires), they can get out of the contract. This does not, however, make the athlete blameless in the signing. And, as a matter of fact, some athletes have taken money from one agent, then signed with another. The agents who have paid for the illegal contract have not done anything to enforce their agreements—other than to threaten the athlete with physical violence.

Summary

Dishonest agents generally exhibit at least one of the following problems:

1. Illegal recruitment of athletes, including early signing.
2. Excessive fees.
3. Conflicts of interest.
4. Incompetence.
5. Mismanagement of the athlete's money.

Footnotes

1. Fred Milverstedt, "Colleges Tackle Unethical Agents," *Athletic Business,* Sept. 1987, p. 24.
2. From *NCAA News,* December 23, 1987.
3. Mike Trope, *Necessary Roughness* (New York: Contemporary Books, 1987), p. 76.
4. From *L.A. Times,* July 23, 1988, p. 1.
5. Milverstedt, "Colleges Tackle Unethical Agents," p. 24.
6. Lionel Sobel, "The Regulation of Sports Agents: An Analytical Primer," *Baylor Law Review* 39: (1987) 719.
7. Milverstedt, "Colleges Tackle Unethical Agents," p. 24.

SIX

Athletes' Considerations in Choosing an Agent

The anonymous survey of college athletes indicated that what they wanted most in an agent was honesty. Those athletes who do not accept illegal bribe money to sign early have their choice of a number of agents or management groups.

It is very shortsighted for an athlete to sign early and should be obvious that he or she is signing with a dishonest person. Athletes who sign early reduce their chances of choosing the agent who will best represent and assist them in their lives and in their careers. No reputable agent jeopardizes an athlete's chance of eligibility or would want him or her to be exposed as a cheater and a fraud.

Keeping Options Open

An Athlete's Contract with the University

An athlete playing for a university and receiving grant-in-aid money has a contract with the university to play according to the NCAA rules and to refrain from jeopardizing that university's standing in athletics.

When an athlete takes money for signing a contract that is in violation of NCAA rules and continues to take grant-in-aid money from the university that is financing his scholarship, the athlete is probably committing fraud against the university. This could be punishable as a misdemeanor. The university could also sue the athlete for lost income from postseason games. A high draft choice who took money illegally might have to pay a great deal of his salary back to the university.

A more serious offense would be for the athlete to fail to list that money as income on his federal income tax return and on state and local returns. This would be both a federal and a state crime.

The Communication with Athletes' Agents

According to NCAA rules an athlete and agent can talk with each other at any time. However, some universities have set up their own rules which may alter this action. Some agents have been banned from some campuses. This, however, has not stopped them from contacting and signing athletes.

No Free Lunch

Athletes must realize that dishonest sports agents are not fairy godfathers. Any money, gifts, or services they give will be taken from the athlete's salary or bonuses—and to a higher degree than the honest agents' rates.

There are many scams that dishonest agents can use to pad their expenses. Some will bring players to their headquarters to work out as soon as their college eligibility is completed. When an agent brings an athlete to his facility to help him get ready to play pro ball he is not doing it out of any other motivation than to enrich his own pockets. The athlete would be better off to stay in school, work for a degree, and work out with the best-prepared people in the country—the college strength coaches.

Dishonest agents have been known to fly across the country to witness the signing of a deed or the purchase of a car. This, of course, is at the expense of the athlete who pays airfare and hourly fees to the agent.

Representing yourself is usually a poor business decision. For the relatively few dollars saved, the athlete can cost himself a great deal in salary and other benefits. Here is an example: In 1980 Cleveland Indians catcher Ron Hassey hit .318. He then negotiated his own contract for $165,000 for the next year. At the same time Yankee catcher Rick Cerone, using an agent, received a salary of $450,000.

Choosing an Agent

Whether or not an athlete is dealing with a dishonest person as his representative can be quickly determined if he is offered money to sign a contract—whether that money comes before or after the athlete's eligibility has ended.

It is obvious that most athletes will want to deal with ethical representatives. This will insure that they will be treated fairly throughout their careers. But greed can get in the way. When an athlete signs an illegal contract prematurely he jeopardizes not only himself but his university.

The first question that must be answered is—Is this agent honest? In our survey of college and professional players, honesty was the number one stated concern of the players. Unhappily, greed often comes into play for many athletes and they take the money to sign.

The Fees

The athlete must evaluate the quality of services against the cost of the agent's fees. While some of the players associations have set maximum fees, there can be hidden costs to an athlete. Some agents charge expenses (phone, travel, etc.) and a few have charged exorbitant and unnecessary fees. Another area of concern for the athlete can be in hidden fees. Some agents have sold insurance and have either kept the commissions (if the agent is an insurance broker or salesman) or have received kickbacks from a broker. Kickbacks have also been given to agents for putting their athletes into business deals such as limited partnerships.

The commissions charged by agents can vary from one or two percent to 10 percent—depending upon the services provided. One agency charges only $5,000 for contract negotiations. Average fees for negotiations only are about three percent or five percent over the minimum salary. Some charge commission on all salary and bonuses; some only on what they negotiate. The professional players associations have often already negotiated minimum salaries for their players. So the agent's job is to get more than the minimum salary and to negotiate signing and incentive bonuses and other financial aspects to the contract.

Some agents use a sliding scale collecting a lesser fee from the higher draft choices. Most charge the same fee for everyone—from five to 10 percent for a total package. With this pay schedule the higher draft choices pay more in total dollars for the same services. (For the fees of some of the more respected agents see the list at the end of Appendix E.)

With existing professionals the fees are generally lower. One management group charges only $5,000 to negotiate the whole contract—even if it is a multiyear contract. They believe that their years of experience in negotiating contracts makes the process relatively easy for most athletes. Other agents charge a percentage of the raise they negotiate. Ten percent of the raise is a common fee. The NBA and NFL players associations set lower maximum fees for contracts negotiated for veteran players.

Fees do not have to be a percentage of income. It is possible to hire a negotiator on an hourly basis; it is also possible to hire someone to negotiate for a flat fee. But with either of these choices the agent gets paid the same even if he does not get the top dollar and this is the reason most athletes choose the percentage fee.

Expenses are charged by some agents. They may charge phone, travel, and hotel expenses in addition to their commissions. The higher commissioned agents are less likely to ask for expenses. Some of the less scrupulous agents have run up many thousands of dollars in unneeded expenses. In one such situation the agent billed the athlete $5,000 in expenses to fly 2,000 miles to stand and watch the signing of an escrow agreement on a home purchase.

Some agents take their fees off the top—from the signing bonuses. Most take it as it is earned by the athlete so that deferred salary to the athlete will also be deferred payment to the agent. The newer and less stable agents are more likely to take their money and run. The athlete should never allow this. The established reputable agents are more likely to take the money as the athlete earns it. Always pay the agent as you are paid.

The NFL Players Association has set maximum fees, which is five percent on any contract for negotiations, for the existing professional players in the union. Rookies are not covered by the union standards; however, the survey of the NFL rookies for the 1988 year showed that most were paying either five percent above the minimum salary or four percent of the total contract for negotiations only.

The NBA Players Association sets a maximum fee of $2,000 for an agent who negotiates only a minimum salary. If the agent negotiates over a minimum salary his maximum fee is set at four percent. The fee is to include only money earned as salary, signing bonus, and performance bonuses. It cannot include other financial gains negotiated, such as insurance policies, loans, automobile, or residence financing.

Checklist for Comparing Management Programs

Selecting an agent or a management group is one of the most important decisions in the life of a young athlete. Every athlete should put a great deal of thought into the decision so that he will be comfortable with his decision.

Using a ten-point scale, rate the factors being considered for your management group. For example, if a person has outstanding qualifications in an area which is very important to you, you might give him a nine or 10. A less qualified person might rate only a two or three or less. If an area is not very important to you but the agent is well qualified you might give the better qualified person a three and a less qualified person a zero or one.

You should keep your ratings private from all agents so that you can be totally objective. Use the following questions to ask more meaningful questions of the person you are interviewing. Make as many notes as you need to get the most accurate picture.

Many players will set up a screening committee to assist them in choosing an agent. They may use an attorney, a business person, and a few trusted friends to help them sort out the best agent or management group. The following questions should be valuable for the athlete or the screening committee to use in evaluating candidates and are also found in Appendix H of this book. (The appendix section can be removed for the athlete's convenience in using it to interview potential agents.)

Questions to Ask When Hiring an Agent

A. Qualifications of negotiator or negotiating team
   1. What expertise does he have in general contract negotiations outside of athletics?
   2. What experience does he have in negotiating for athletes?
   3. What type of expertise does he have in contract law in general?
   4. Is he registered with the NCAA?
   5. Is he registered with the players association for his sport?
   6. Is the certification permanent or annual?
   7. How long has he been in business?
   8. Have there been any complaints to the players union about this agent?
   9. Has the agent provided his educational credentials?
   10. Has the agent provided references?

B. Qualifications of the money management team
   1. Is the representative a C.F.A. (Chartered Financial Analyst—the highest rating in the field)?
   2. Is agent a CFP (certified financial planner—an easy license used primarily by insurance salesmen)?
   3. Does he have special expertise: in banking? in securities? in real estate?
   4. Is he a "hands-on" manager (whereas he handles your money)?
   5. Is he "hands-off" (whereas you control your money)?
   6. Is a financial plan developed?
   7. What does the financial plan cost you?
   8. How is the financial plan developed?
   9. Does agent ever take commissions or kickbacks on financial dealings he arranges with you, such as: insurance sales? limited partnerships? sale of stocks or bonds?
   10. Does he sell any kind of insurance?
   11. Will he ever ask for a power of attorney to make your investments?

C. The qualifications of the tax-planning person
   1. Is he a certified public accountant (CPA)?

2. What is the strength of his company?
3. What experience has he had with the special tax problems of athletes?

D. Strength analysis before pro camp
1. Does agent do film analysis to discover your strengths and weaknesses so that you can work to improve yourself before the pro camp?
2. Who does the film analysis?
3. What are his qualifications?
4. What sort of report does he develop?
5. What are the qualifications of the person making the recommendations?
6. How does the agent get you into camp?
7. What are his contacts?

E. Available experts
1. What types of experts are available to you through the agent?
2. Is there a charge for these services?

F. Evaluation of honesty of agent
1. Did the agent offer you money before your eligibility was completed? (*This is unethical and illegal under the criminal code.*)
2. Did he offer you money (such as a loan) to sign? (*This is unethical and a breach of contract law under the civil codes.*)
3. Have any complaints ever been lodged against him? (Check with the player association.)
4. If he is going to handle any money, is he bonded?

G. Contract structure
1. How is the contract structured?
2. What provisions are inserted to protect you?

H. Education interest
1. Does he ask you to drop out of school?
2. Is he interested in helping you get your degree?

I. Financial problems
1. If you need money early, how is it handled?
2. If you want insurance, what does he do?
3. If you want a car, how does he help you?
4. Does agent provide any special banking services?
5. What do the special banking services cost?

J. Agent's fees
1. What money must agent pay for your well-being?
2. What are agent's fees?
3. Do agent fees cover: negotiating? daily accounting? doing all taxes? private banking? financial planning? investment recommendations?
4. Does he charge you expenses for: phone? travel?

K. Endorsements
1. What are the possibilities of endorsements?
2. What would you need to do to get endorsement money?
3. What record does agent have in getting endorsements for his players?
4. What is agent's program for making you marketable?

L. Retirement
1. Does agent have a retirement plan available?
2. How is the retirement plan structured?

M. Agent's strengths
1. Does agent emphasize that he is better because he is small or local?
2. Does he have regional representatives so that wherever you play you will have a personal contact?
3. Is he available through an (800) line at no cost to you?
4. Does he have special expertise in athletics?
5. Does he have strong contacts with both the professional leagues?

N. Agent's special services
1. Does he provide special services for: psychologist? marriage counselor? weight training and conditioning specialists? other?

O. Special considerations
1. Is the agent one who is interested in the long-term goals of the athlete?
2. What are agent's fees?
3. What do agent's fees cover?
4. Are the fees paid: up front? as earned?
5. Are all of the agent's expenses covered in the fees?
6. Are the fees billed: as a percentage of income? as a flat fee? as an hourly fee?
7. Overall, how do you rate agent's qualifications, services, and concern?

The Other Intangibles

Being a Friend

In addition to the business side of the relationship it is a real bonus if the athlete and agent are friends. There are many times when an athlete needs a confidant for his personal and professional problems. He needs someone to cheer him up at times. And at other times he needs someone to whom he can tell the truth—even if it hurts.

Knowledge of the Life of an Athlete

Athletes live differently from other people. They may be traded from team to team. They may have extra pressures from "athletic groupies" who are willing to give sexual favors to an important athlete. There may be more free time. This combined with the added pressures may increase an athlete's need for feeling relief perhaps by using alcohol or other drugs.

Professional sports agents are aware of these problems and can aid the athlete in adjusting to his life in professional sports.

The Agent's Reputation with the Teams

Many teams will bypass an athlete if he is represented by one of the agents who is not well thought of. Some agents go into the negotiation arena with unrealistic expectations and demands. The teams will refuse to pay more than their top dollar budgeted. This will result in holdouts or in late reporting—which hurts the team.

While you do not want an agent who has more allegiance to management than to his players, you also do not want one who is disliked by the team management. The facts are that there are many players who are so close in ability that one small factor may make a difference as to where, or if, a player is drafted. And for every spot from which a player is dropped in the draft there is a significant financial loss.

Summary

The athlete needs an agent to increase his chances of getting the best possible compensation for his services and to increase his chances of making good use of his money. However, choosing an agent is not as easy as it may seem.

Most people, especially those uninitiated in the business world, are especially gullible. They can easily be taken in by the lies and the false promises of the unethical agents. The agents promising something for nothing should be eliminated from consideration immediately. Anyone asking an athlete to break the rules is not honest and likely will not become honest later.

Once you have narrowed the choice to the ethical agents they should be evaluated in terms of: contract expertise, financial plans, tax reduction, and the other factors that go into the business dealings of a professional athlete.

SEVEN

Regulation of Agents by Colleges and Associations

Several organizations attempt to regulate the conduct of agents. The NCAA has its ideas. The players associations have rules. Some agents have their own association—the Association for Representatives of Professional Athletes and there is also the Sports Lawyers Association. Several states have laws that apply to the ethical and legal conduct of agents and individual schools often have committees or rules that are supposed to govern the conduct of agents.

Our surveys have indicated that the coaches and athletic directors suggest for regulation everything from NCAA and professional league certification to state and federal laws. The agents surveyed generally prefer a federal law. Having to abide by the laws of each state as statutes are enacted is too cumbersome, and with bonds being required in each state, too costly. Most agents and other legal experts favor federal laws.

Obeying the Rules and Laws

The problem with sports agents is not the ethical group who obeys the laws and rules but rather the unethical agents. According to John Levins, former head of the NCAA legislative services, "You can put as many regulations on the books as you want, but what you'll find is that the reputable agents will pay attention to it, the disreputable agents will ignore it, and the reputable agents will end up at a greater disadvantage than they were to begin with."[1]

Control by the Colleges

Many of the athletic directors and coaches do not cooperate with agents by giving out information about their players. Most will forward mail to the players; however, a few have withheld the mail until the season was completed.

Many colleges do not allow agents on the campus. Some will allow certified agents to meet with the campus panels who advise the senior athletes and may recommend agents to players.

Most of the coaches surveyed do not cooperate with agents unless they are certified and the coach is notified. A few will help set up interviews with certified agents if they feel it is their duty to help the athlete in getting set to play professional sports. There was general agreement that agents should register on the campus but should not appear on the campus until after the season is completed.

NCAA Rules and Suggestions

Counseling for the Athlete

The NCAA has asked each university to set up a committee of three advisors to assist the athletes in counseling a potential professional athlete and in choosing an agent. The committee should be composed of two nonathletic department personnel and one person from the athletic department. This committee should develop information from all sources (i.e., lawyers, financial consultants, professional teams, players associations, and player agents). As of 1989 there were over 70 universities that have set up such committees.

Agent-Athlete Communication

The NCAA rules do not prohibit contacts between an agent and an athlete but they do prohibit any agreement being made between them. It does not matter whether the agreement is verbal or written because either way it is a contract. An agreement is against NCAA rules even if there is no compensation.

If an athlete and an agent reach an agreement prior to the termination of the athlete's NCAA eligibility, that athlete will be ineligible from further NCAA competition. Consequently, any games in which he plays can be forfeited. Even if the contract is not legally enforceable it results in loss of college eligibility for the player in that sport.

Compensation or the Promise of Compensation

Acceptable compensation for an athlete under NCAA rules includes:

1. Scholarships or grants-in-aid, from the university that are within the rules of the NCAA.
2. Financial reimbursement from the United States Olympic Committee to cover financial loss for preparing for and competing in the Olympic Games.
3. Borrowing against future earnings from an accredited financial lending institution. Borrowed money can only be used to buy insurance (with no cash surrender value) against injury that would prevent the athlete from pursuing a career as a professional athlete. No third party (including members of the athletic department) may be involved in helping to secure the loan. Any athlete who borrows money for this purpose must report the transaction to the school and file the proper papers.

Illegal compensation for an athlete includes, but is not limited to:

1. Salary, gifts, gratuities, some loans, etc., paid to the athlete or to other people, such as family members, who are intimately associated with the athlete.
2. Excessive awards, expenses, or benefits.
3. Expenses received from an outside amateur sports team or organization in excess of actual and necessary travel and meal expenses for practice or game competition.
4. Professional services given to an athlete free or at reduced cost. This constitutes pay unless those same services are available to the student body in general.

Relations with Professional Teams

Under NCAA rules, if an athlete has been a professional in one sport and returns to college, he cannot become an amateur in that sport. However, he can be an amateur in any other sport.

Athletes may try out for a professional team during the summer or during a semester in which he is not a full-time student. However, he can try out only once for each team. The visit to the team cannot exceed 48 hours and the compensation for that visit cannot exceed actual expenses.

An athlete may inquire about being accepted in the professional draft (e.g, a fifth-year senior or a possible hardship case). However, if he actually puts his name up for the draft he will then become ineligible for college play in that sport. This holds true even if he later takes his name off the draft list.

Rules of Players Associations

Players associations were formed to work for the interests of the players, particularly in collective bargaining agreements with the league. These associations can negotiate to set minimum salaries, retirement benefits, agent fees, agent conduct, and a great number of other issues. Some players associations regulate the contract advisor by certifying him; some require certification before any contract can be negotiated. Other unions, such as that of the National Football League, do not require certification of agents handling rookies. Several of the agents surveyed believe that the players unions should certify all agents—those representing both rookies and veterans.

National Football League Players Association (NFLPA)

The following information reflects the terms of the 1982 collective bargaining agreement; however, there may be changes following litigation and if a new bargaining agreement is reached.

Certification

Agents who wish to represent existing professionals may apply for *certification* with the National Football League Players Association. Certification, which can be provisional or permanent, allows the agent to deal with existing professional athletes. Agents who represent only rookies need not be certified. Of the approximately 500 agents certified with the NFLPA, only about 30 are permanently certified.

To become certified an agent must submit an extensive application and attend a yearly seminar that is sponsored by the NFLPA. Most college football coaches prefer to work with NFL-certified agents. However, Joe Paterno, while agreeing that such certification is good, notes that many good agents are not certified.

Compensation

An agent can collect fees on the following: the player's salary in the amount that exceeds the minimum salary, the signing bonus, reporting bonus, and negotiated incentives. (A *negotiated incentive* might include payment for a certain number of passes caught, yards gained, or sacks made.) Agent fees cannot include honor bonuses (money paid to Rookie of the Year or All-Pro selections) or any money earned by the player which was part of the union's collective bargaining agreement.

Allowable Fees and Salary

Allowable fees for negotiation are set at a maximum of five percent for each year of the contract negotiated. If an agent is not able to negotiate more than the minimum salary for his client, his fee will be $125 per hour or $1,000—whichever is less. And this fee is paid only if the player makes the active list and plays one regular season game. In addition to these fees the agent (contract advisor) can collect expenses such as telephone and travel expenses, if approved in advance by the player.

Higher fees are possible if the agent has put in extraordinary time or has done an exceptional job of negotiating for the player. The agent must apply to the NFLPA for a higher fee and the amount must be approved by the player.

At the present time certification of the agent is not necessary for the first contract; consequently, many first-year contract representatives are not qualified or honest. These are the people who are doing most of the dishonest recruiting of the college athletes.

The agent can collect his fees only when the player receives his salary. In the case of deferred salary, the agent collects only if and when the player is paid.

For rookies the minimum salary is $50,000 and is increased by $10,000 for each successive year, reaching a maximum of $200,000 after 16 years.

National Basketball Players Association (NBPA)

The NBPA's regulation of agents is more complete than that of the NFLPA—the NBPA regulations governing player agents include representing rookies as well as veterans.

The NBPA has standards that include the prohibition of an agent offering a college or professional athlete money, or anything of value, in order to be his agent. This rule also applies to the offering of gifts to family members of the athlete.

Allowable Fees

Allowable fees for agents are also set by the NBPA. If an agent negotiates a contract that is only for the minimum compensation allowed to a professional basketball player, the fee is set at $2,000. If the agent negotiates a contract in excess of the minimum contract that has been negotiated between the players association and the league, the fee is four percent.

The agent fee is based upon the player's salary, signing bonus, and any financial incentives actually received. It cannot include other considerations from the clubs, such as the value of a loan from the team to the player, the value of an insurance policy, or the value of an automobile or a residence.

National Hockey League Players Association (NHLPA)

The National Hockey League Players Association does not have a certification for players or a limitation on agent fees at this time. However, because of past occurrences of agents monetarily defrauding players, the NHLPA is looking into requiring qualifications of agents who seek to represent NHL members. Two agents have been jailed during the past 10 years for fraudulent activities relating to hockey players.

The minimum salary of hockey players in the National Hockey League is $25,000 and $18,000 for those players in the minor leagues.

Other financial incentives already negotiated by the players association include:

an additional $5,000 for each player on the first-place team in each division

$2,500 for each on the second-place teams

payment of $3,000 to the losers in the division semifinals

$6,000 to the losers of the finals

$11,000 to the losers of the conference championship

$18,000 to the losers of the Stanley Cup Championship

$25,000 to the winners of the Stanley Cup

$3,000 prizes for the winners of each trophy

$1,000 prizes for the runners-up

Major League Baseball Players Association (MLBPA)

Agents must be certified by the association. There are no maximum fees set.

The Canadian Football League

For certification the Canadian Football League requires an application and a fee of $200. If the contract advisor is to handle the player's funds the advisor must be bonded. The maximum fee for first-year negotiations is seven percent of the minimum salary. Maximum fee for the second year is four percent in excess of the minimum salary. The third-year fee is two percent in excess of the minimum salary. The rules stipulate that the contract advisor cannot be paid until the player is paid. A contract advisor may charge an hourly fee but must advise the player on what the maximum fee will be.

The Canadian Football League rules prohibit a contract advisor from offering anything of value to a player in order to represent him. There is also the rule against offering anything of value to another person (family member, friend) in order to represent the player.

Professional Golf Association Tour

This association does not deal with agent and player relations. Their only responsibility is to regulate the professional golf tour. Golfers are, therefore, on their own in dealing with agents. If they have any problems they must use the court system for settling their grievances.

Association of Representatives of Professional Athletes (ARPA)

This association was formed in 1978 with the assistance of the National Football League Players Association. It is devoted to maintaining the highest degree of integrity and competence in representing the professional athlete.

The Code of Ethics of the ARPA includes the following:

1. The representative can never accept payment from a professional team or its representative. He must always hold the interests of his client primary.
2. The representative shall not offer, promise, or provide financial support of any kind to the athlete, his family members, his coaches, or any college employee in order to become the agent of an athlete.

Regulation of Agents by the Players Associations

Some coaches and agents, as well as some players associations, would like to regulate agents through the players associations. These associations are close to the players and may get accurate information more quickly than state or federal governments could. If all agents had to be certified by the associations in order to represent any athlete, regulation could come quickly. The major problem is that these associations do not have a great inclination to punish the incompetents or the dishonest agents. When they do they must move through governmental channels.

A major problem with this proposed solution is that it may be in violation of federal antitrust law which "prohibits contracts that restrain trade."[2] The same is true of the NCAA rules.[3]

Identifying the Unethical Agents

It would be beneficial if, whenever an athlete was approached by an unethical agent, he would reject the offer and then report the incident to the athletic department, the NCAA, and the player's union. Unfortunately, this is seldom done. It usually takes a great deal of mishandling of funds before the athlete gets upset. The fact that the loans the dishonest agent gives him result in a much higher fee structure and the fact that the athlete actually loses money in the long run are seldom enough for the dishonest athlete to turn down the unethical agent.

Often agents keep files on other agents. Once they sign an athlete who has been approached by a dishonest agent, and possibly taken money, the honest agent may report the suspected agent to the NCAA, the university, or the players association. When enough evidence is gathered a civil court action may commence. And at times there are criminal violations of law that have developed.

A sting operation has been suggested by which an athlete would be rewarded for revealing a dishonest agent. The problem arises in determining what type of reward would be legal and appropriate—whatever it was it would not approach the thousands of dollars the athlete could collect from the agent. Another problem that may result is the violence or the threat of violence that could be (and has been) used to keep the athlete quiet.

Summary

Agents are regulated by several of their own organizations, the NCAA, and the players unions. Each organization has different rules. None of the organizations have the clout of law or the power to subpoena. While some agents would like the unions to have some control over the agents, it has been difficult to achieve at this time.

Footnotes

1. Fred Milverstedt, "Colleges Tackle Unethical Agents," *Athletic Business,* Sept. 1987, p. 26.

2. Lionel Sobel, "The Regulation of Sports Agents: An Analytical Primer," *Baylor Law Review* 39 (1987): 727.

3. Sobel, "Regulation of Sports Agents," p. 728.

EIGHT

Legal Regulations
State and Federal Legislation

Don Canham, former athletic director at Michigan, has said that we need state laws to control the actions of athletic agents. The NCAA has no subpoena power so they cannot put people under oath to testify.

Several states have enacted or are in the process of enacting legislation to regulate sports agents and management groups. The federal government has investigated the possibility but has yet to pass a law.

State or federal legislation would have three advantages over the nonlegislative regulations under which agents now work.

1. It would require that all agents in all sports be bound by the same rules.
2. Criminal sanctions would be more easily administered so that there would be "teeth" in the regulations.
3. The tested enforcement mechanisms of laws would be more threatening to dishonest agents than is the threat of enforcement by the nonlegislative organizations.[1]

With state or federal legislation, athletics would be subpoenaed and would therefore have to testify under oath. The penalty of perjury may encourage those testifying to report facts that would otherwise be hidden.

State Laws

California enacted the first regulations for sports agents in 1981. About 20 states have followed. These laws, in general, have been enacted to add support to the NCAA rules and to protect the colleges. They generally address the issues caused by the unethical agents who sign football and basketball players early but there is little mention about agents in other sports. The laws may also address the issue of mismanagement of funds and often require a financial bond to be posted.

At this time no educational requirements or testing are required to become an agent—a high school dropout could qualify![2]

The laws affecting agents take two approaches. California, Oklahoma, Louisiana, Texas, Alabama, Iowa, and Georgia require that all agents register in the state. Ohio, Indiana, Minnesota, Tennessee, and Kentucky have established laws concerning the early signing of athletes and set penalties for those who break the law.

Another difference in the direction of the laws is found in who is included in the scope of the law. Some states include all agents; others exclude attorneys who practice as agents.

Some states (Georgia, Minnesota, and Tennessee) have only civil penalties for signing an athlete early. A civil suit might be initiated if an athlete is declared ineligible because of signing a contract with an agent before he was allowed to do so by the NCAA. The injured party, such as a university, can sue for lost ticket sales, lost television revenue, and lost revenue for not being able to qualify for postseason events. A university could also sue for damages for recovery of the money that the university spent on the athletic scholarship.

Some states (Louisiana, Kentucky, and Indiana) have only criminal penalties. In Indiana and Kentucky the "failure to disclose the recruitment of a student athlete" is a Class D felony. In Louisiana the agent can be fined up to $10,000 and sentenced to prison for up to a year.

The other states have both civil and criminal penalties. In addition to the penalties some states require that an agent be bonded. The high amount of the bonds required—up to $100,000 per state—has made it difficult for agents to obtain bonding.[3] This puts an additional burden on the legitimate agents and is reflected in their fees to the athletes.

Some states limit the amount of the fee that can be charged the athlete. Some will also limit the amount to be paid to an agent in any one year. This has the effect of making it impossible for the agent to take all of his commission up front.

Employees of players associations have often worked second jobs as sports agents. This practice, which might be viewed as a conflict of interest, has been prohibited by the California and Alabama laws.

California Law

California was the first state to enact a law affecting sports agents. This was done in 1981 and amended in 1986. It requires that agents submit a certificate of completion of their education, training, and experience relating to contract negotiation, contract law, arbitration, complaint resolution, or civil resolution of contract disputes. However, it sets no minimum standards or testing to ascertain the agent's level of expertise as is done for most other professions in the state (i.e., building contractors, marriage counselors, and lawyers).

The law applies only to those who negotiate contracts. It does not apply to those handling money or advising on investments.[4] Agents must be registered with the Labor Commissioner or any contracts are void and unenforceable. California lawyers who are members of the State Bar Association are not required to register but are bound by the law.

The law does not expressly cover agents who merely conduct contract negotiations in California or whose clients live in California or are employed by California teams. However, the Labor Commissioner considers the act to cover not only agents with a residence in California but also out-of-state agents with client athletes living or working in the state. This, however, will probably be challenged by an out-of-state agent if he is charged under the law.[5]

Agents must post a $25,000 bond and pay a minimum of $500 in annual fees. They are also limited to a 10 percent maximum fee from their clients. The law also specifies that an agent cannot pay an employee of the educational institution for referring clients. By the end of 1988 only 21 agents had applied.

Oklahoma Law

Oklahoma also requires the registration of all sports agents. Their requirements are similar to California's except that they add they want training and experience for agents in federal income taxation and in federal estate planning. They require an annual $1,000 fee and higher bond—$100,000—and they do not exclude lawyers from the law's provisions.

Oklahoma also codifies some of the NCAA rules, such as not paying university employees for referring an athlete, not offering anything of value to an athlete to sign a contract, and not entering an oral or written agreement with the athlete until his collegiate eligibility is completed. Like the California law, it affects only those who do contract negotiation, not those who handle money or advise on investments.

Texas Law

Texas passed their Athlete Agent Act in 1987. It requires an annual $1,000 registration fee. It also requires a $100,000 bond if the agent performs financial services other than just contract negotiation. The law affects only agents dealing with college athletes, not with those whose only dealings are with established professionals.

Other States

Other states with agent regulation laws on the books (as of January 1989) include: Louisiana, Alabama, Ohio, Iowa, Indiana, Georgia, Kentucky, Minnesota, and Tennessee. Another 15 to 20 states are considering laws.

Problems with the Laws

A problem with some of the laws is that they refer only to college athletes. But since high school baseball and hockey players sometimes turn professional as soon as they leave high school, the legislation may not cover them. Also, college baseball, basketball, and hockey players may be prevented from obtaining agent representation even though they are legally drafted by a professional team.[6] It is only the NFL and the NBA that have rules prohibiting the signing of athletes before they have completed their first four years of college.

The laws are aimed primarily at illegal signings of football and basketball players. They do not generally protect existing professionals in contract negotiations, nor do they usually protect the athlete's financial interests from money handling or investment decisions.

Another problem with the various state laws is that many agents operate in all or most states. They are therefore involved in interstate commerce and should be governed by federal laws. Most professions operating in a state are entirely local (i.e., doctors, lawyers, builders) so state regulation is appropriate.

As an example of the complexity of the problem, who do you think would have jurisdiction in the following case? *A football player who played four years for the University of Oklahoma and who is drafted by the Houston Oilers is contacted by an agent who lives in New Jersey but has an office in New York. They meet at the athlete's parents' house in Los Angeles to discuss signing with the agent.* If problems arose in the relationship between the athlete and the agent it would probably have to be settled by the Federal District Court. It may well be that the states are legislating interstate commerce and have no right to do so—since this right is reserved for Congress. There have been attempts at federal regulation but they have not yet been successful.

The Case for Federal Regulation

Professional athletic teams span the nation and are truly involved in interstate commerce. Agents and colleges are found in all states. State laws have taken varying approaches to handling dishonorable sports agents. The result is that a problem of national scope exists but the federal government is not ready to regulate it.

It seems that the federal government is the only body that can effectively regulate the problems involving professional athletics. With nearly half of the states either passing laws or developing them, it will make it nearly impossible for the legitimate agents to comply with the registration fees and the bonding fees in each state. This denies athletes of the best possible selection of management representatives.

It is the consensus of sports lawyers that national control is the best avenue. With national control, as with state control, there is subpoena power and there is the real threat of punishment for offenders. Without some form of legal control it is much easier for the unscrupulous agents to break the rules established by the NCAA, the colleges, and the players associations. If these quasi-official organizations want justice they are required to file civil suits against the agents and they often feel it is not worth the trouble.

In 1976 the House Select Committee on Professional Sports stated that "the role of the player agent is . . . a matter of Federal concern,"[7] but that a "successor committee undertake an investigation to determine the nature and scope of abuses of the agent-client relationship in professional sports, the appropriateness of Federal involvement in this area, and the need for protective legislation."[8]

Federal regulation and enforcement could be financed by fees from the agents. It would therefore be self-supporting and would not cost the taxpayer anything.

"Regulation of agents has got to become Federal law," said Frank Windegger, athletic director at TCU. He had just lost two athletes who had signed illegally with Jim Abernethy.[9]

A Proposal

A federal law should state the requirements for certification by the Department of Commerce. The requirements for certification should include:

1. A bachelor's degree from an accredited college.
2. A demonstrated knowledge of contract law, knowledge of investments, and knowledge of taxation. These could be tested by written examination.
3. Posting of a bond of at least $50,000 or an appropriate level of malpractice insurance.

4. No evidence of a criminal background.

The law should also address:

1. A maximum annual fee that could be charged the athlete for the following: contract negotiation, tax services, financial services, and endorsement contracts.
2. Penalties for signing scholarship athletes to contracts before their eligibility has expired.
3. Penalties for signing illegal contracts.
4. Penalties for giving gifts or making loans to the athlete or to the athlete's family or friends as an inducement to sign a contract.
5. Invoking the Constitution's "supremacy clause" and invalidating the existing state laws.
6. Funding for the administration and enforcement of the law supported by fees from players associations, the NCAA, and agents.
7. Provision for both civil and criminal penalties.
8. Inclusion of all agents for all sports.
9. Whether the federal government or the players associations will set the certification standards for the representation of their athletes.

Summary

In an attempt to brace the regulations affecting sports agents, states have enacted various laws. However, the laws vary considerably from state to state. It is time for the federal government to step into the arena and regulate this national business.

Footnotes

1. David Dunn, "Regulation of Sports Agents: Since at First It Hasn't Succeeded, Try Federal Regulation," *Hastings Law Journal* 19 (1988): 1049.
2. Lionel Sobel, "The Regulation of Sports Agents," *Athletic Business,* Sept. 1987, p. 746.
3. Glenn Wong, "States Are Getting Tough with Agents," *Athletic Business,* August, 1988, p. 18.

4. Dunn, "Regulation of Sports Agents," pp. 1050–1052.

5. Dunn, "Regulation of Sports Agents," pp. 1052–1053.

6. Glenn Wong, "Agent Legislation Differs among States," *Athletic Business,* September, 1988, p. 20.

7. "Inquiry Into Professional Sports," Final Report of the Select Committee on Professional Sports. House of Representatives, H. R. Rep. No. 94, 94th Congress, Second Session (1977), p. 7.

8. U.S. House of Representatives, "Inquiry into Professional Sports," p. 79.

9. "Former Sports Agent Charges College Players Signed Contracts," *U.S.A. Today,* Dec. 16, 1987, p. C9.

NINE

Developing a Program for Educating the Athlete

It is in the interest of the university as well as of the athlete to develop an educational program to alert the athlete to the advantages and the disadvantages of working with an agent. Certainly no university wants to forfeit games or gate receipts. Having a football player declared ineligible because of an early signing and having to forfeit games and a chance at a postseason bowl game can cost the university over a million dollars. And in college basketball ineligibility for the NCAA playoffs can also cost the school a great deal of money.

In the interest of fairness the university should be clear in telling the potential professional athlete the advantages and disadvantages of accepting a college scholarship. Each sport carries different potentials for becoming a professional. It must be brought to the attention of the athlete that when accepting an athletic scholarship he is signing a contract with the university. Each year the athlete signs a new scholarship offer so that, in effect, he or she is obligated to play for only that one year. There are other options to accepting the scholarship.

Educating the High School Athlete

The high school coach is perhaps more knowledgeable about the potential future of the athlete than anyone else. The coach should therefore be ready to counsel the athlete on the pros and cons of accepting a college scholarship and the terms of that contract. The college recruiter should also make the athlete understand the sanctity of a contract and the ways that some unscrupulous agents will attempt to get him to break the contract.

Most athletes who accept college scholarships will never make it at the professional level. Even those who can play professional sports will generally profit from a college education. Consequently, it is a great advantage to the average scholarship athlete to be able to attend a university. The scholarship certainly has a great monetary value to the scholarship-athlete. The yearly tuition can range from $2,000 to $10,000 and the room and board offered can add another $4,000 to $8,000. Then the expected annual income from a post-college occupation outside of professional sports will add several thousand dollars per year to the income of the college graduate over that of a high school graduate.

It is a sad comment that many college athletes either do not have the interest or the ability to profit from a college education. Many colleges, even those considered highly academic, often fabricate college majors that will be useless to the student-athlete. College majors in stadium management, general studies, recreation, criminal justice, physical education, black studies, business, and other areas can be made very simple or very difficult. One major western university has a very difficult physical education major but an easy business major. The marginal student-athletes usually enroll in business or sociology at that school. A major southern university, renowned for its academic tradition, hides its marginal academically capable athletes in a major titled "Stadium Management." One may wonder just how many stadia there are to manage in this country.

Available Options

Outlining the options available to the athlete can probably best be accomplished by the high school coach who is more likely to have the best interests of the athlete at heart. The options are different for each sport.

Football Scholarships

Football scholarships require that the athlete wait at least four years before becoming eligible for participation in the National Football League. Options available for the athlete who does not wish to finish his college contract would be to play semi-professional football until the four years has expired.

Another option that is being discussed in a new spring professional league is to allow players to play professional football in that league but to give scholarships to those players so that they can complete high school or college while playing in the league. (While the league has been in development since the USFL folded, at this writing the league is not yet off the ground.) The idea of having a place to perfect the skills of the game and to play, other than at a college, is a real possibility and could be done at the professional or semi-professional level in the United States or in Europe.

There is no question that at this time the level of coaching at the college and university levels is far superior to that available at the semi-professional level. Colleges also give the athlete the opportunity to avail himself of the best in weight training facilities.

Basketball Scholarships

Basketball scholarships also bind the athlete to the college and keep the National Basketball Association away from the player for four years unless there is a case made for "hardship" by the athlete.

For the outstanding high school basketball player there is the chance to be signed by the NBA, like Moses Malone and Darryl Dawkins were. There is also the chance to play in a lower level professional league, like the Continental League, or to play professional basketball in Europe. Such options require "connections" with the professional basketball world and, generally speaking, the well-known college player has a far greater chance to be taken by a professional league than would a high school player.

Just as with football, the caliber of coaching available in college is better than that available in the lower professional leagues. The four years of strength training and basketball competition in college will generally make the athlete a far better player who is more likely to make it in the professional ranks.

Other Sports Options

Baseball and hockey players are allowed to leave high school or college and play because the professional baseball leagues have never taken the "hands-off" approach that the football and basketball leagues have adopted. The National Hockey League rule allows for any player over 18 to be taken in the June draft. College baseball players can be accepted into the professional ranks after they are 21 years old, or 120 days after they have withdrawn from their college, or, if in a four-year college, after the junior year. Junior college athletes can be taken at any time. Tennis players and golfers can turn professional at any time.

NCAA Suggestions

Problems relating to college scholarships primarily concern football and basketball athletes, since other athletes either have no professional opportunities (i.e., swimmers, wrestlers, gymnasts) or can turn pro at any time (i.e., golfers, baseball and tennis players).

The NCAA could consider developing a clearly written, simplified form that would explain the nature of the contract with the university and how signing with an agent early can be a violation of that contract. This letter would be signed along with the letter of intent. Civil penalties for violation of the terms might even be included in the contract. A similar form should be signed by the parents or guardian of the player. Another possibility may be a contract with the NCAA signed by both the athlete and his parents or guardian.

Points covered by the letter or contract may include the following:

I. The scholarship is a contract with the university.
   A. Obligations of the university
      1. To provide an education
      2. To provide room and board for the athlete
      3. To honor the contract even if the athlete is injured
      4. To provide tutors as needed to improve academic achievement
   B. Obligations of the athlete
      1. To play for that university
      2. To remain eligible to play by
         a) Keeping the grade average sufficiently high
         b) Refraining from breaking NCAA rules
         c) Not making oral or written commitments to sign with an agent
         d) Accepting nothing of value except that provided by the university

II. A violated contract may result in civil penalties.

III. Federal penalties for tax evasion will result if he does not report all income to the federal government. (Illegal payments by dishonest agents are really advances on future income.)

Programs of the University's Athletic Department

Programs for informing the athlete of the mutual aspects of the contract with the university should begin at the time of the signing of the letter of intent. This should include the information previously outlined.

Many colleges have some type of program for the scholarship athletes each year. This should become standard operating procedure for every college that offers athletic scholarships. Some colleges offer the same program to all athletes each year; others tailor the program to the type of athlete and the year of participation. Suggestions for a program follow.

Freshmen

Freshmen should have the rules and laws clarified and then be tested on them. They should be instructed on contracts in general and, later, on the specifics of the contract between the player and the school. A law school professor or a professor of business law is the ideal source person for this aspect of the program.

The specifics of the contract between the athlete and the college and the rules of the NCAA should be clarified by the athletic director or representative. This aspect of the program should stress the penalties of signing another contract for athletic services and should include the problems of the loss of income for the university when an athlete is found ineligible and postseason games are forfeited. It should also bring to the attention of the athletes that the university could sue the athlete and possibly collect from his professional salary and signing bonus. The federal penalties for nonreporting of income should also be noted.

Options for the player for earning additional money could be developed at this time. There should also be a place for the athlete to come to for financial counseling should problems occur in his life or in the life of his family.

Players should be asked to report any illegal contacts and contract offers to the athletic department. Rumors abound in agent circles about certain top basketball players who have been signed since they entered college. Usually they sign with "family friends"—in actuality people they probably did not know before their senior season in high school.

Sophomores

Sophomores can be exposed to the same type of program. Contracts in general and the NCAA rules should be discussed. Many outstanding sophomores are approached by dishonest agents to sign illegally.

Juniors

Juniors are more likely to be contacted by dishonest agents. While the contacts have been happening earlier and earlier, most are not contacted until after spring practice at the end of the junior year. The same type of information on contracts and NCAA rules should be repeated.

Some information on the professional draft and the programs of agents could be introduced at this time. The athletes are probably thinking about it so it is a good time to introduce some of the information they will need when they are ready for the professional game.

The information needed could include general information on negotiation and financial packages available. The emphasis should be on the fact that there is much more to finding a good agent or management group than just signing a contract and hoping that the agent will do the best job possible. Athletes should be made aware that there is a big difference in the type of representation possible.

Seniors

Seniors have to be reminded of the rules but they also need much more information on what to look for in an agent. They should be cautioned about making any commitments during the time they still have eligibility in a sport. Once the senior season is completed someone should take responsibility for educating the potential professionals about their options. The coaches are generally busy recruiting the next year's freshmen class so they may not be of great help at this time. A representative of the athletic department should be placed in charge of this project and it should be coordinated with a career counseling panel appointed from outside the athletic department.

Special Counseling Panels

The NCAA has suggested that special panels advise potential professional athletes. It recommends that the panel be selected by the chief executive officer of the university. It should be made up of employees from outside the athletic department. The panel should "obtain information and expertise from a variety of sources (e.g., lawyers, financial consultants, professional sports teams, player associations, and player agents) in an effort to provide objective information about professional career opportunities and evaluate the various services and proposals extended by player agents."[1] Over 70 universities have set up such panels.

Counseling of the potential professional should begin immediately after the last game of the season. Agents will have already contacted the athlete. This is legal. At the postseason games, such as the Shrine and Hula Bowls for football players, there will be many agents talking with the athletes. The athletes will be eager to talk with the agents—as they should be. But the athletes should have some good questions and a degree of skepticism as they talk with their potential agents.

The checklist of questions in Chapter 6 will give the career panel a good outline for evaluating the offerings of various agents or management groups. The panel might also look at just the agents who are listed with the NCAA, although there are competent agents who have not chosen to be listed.

The career counseling panels can verify the academic and professional credentials of the agents they are evaluating. There are a few who profess to have academic degrees or professional expertise which, in truth, they do not possess. Look for legitimately earned degrees such as Doctor of Jurisprudence or Ph.D. Look for accreditation in the State Bar Association or for the legitimacy of a CPA (certified public accountant) or C.F.A. (Chartered Financial Analyst). Do not be fooled by such appellations as CFP (the easy-to-obtain certified financial planner) or other lesser qualifications.

Summary

High school and college coaches and school administration all have an obligation to make clear the elements of the contract with the school and with contract law. The athlete must understand the importance of signing a contract for a scholarship with the university. It is in the interest of both the college and the athlete to continue an education program relative to honest and dishonest representation.

Footnotes

1. NCAA memorandum to individuals acting in the capacity of player agents, Sept. 2, 1988.

TEN

Possible Solutions to the Problem of Dishonest and Incompetent Agents

Coaches Recommendations

The coaches surveyed cited several considerations for regulation. Some wanted agents to be certified and registered with the NCAA and the NFLPA. Some wanted the agents to appear before a college panel so that they could be approved by the college (if so qualified). Some coaches wanted state regulations; others suggested minimum education and licensing requirements, such as expertise in contract law and in finances.

One interesting suggestion was in having the NFL set a salary standard for each position in each round of the draft. At the time of this writing there is a strong possibility that this will happen very soon for football. Negotiation on salary would then be unnecessary. (However, since other areas are included in contract negotiation, perhaps an agent will be necessary to handle other areas, such as deferred payment, incentives, loans, etc.)

Coaches' suggestions for qualifications included: a law degree; expertise in taxes, investments, and contracts; and a rating system combining the ratings of the players, the universities, the NCAA, and professional athlete players associations.

Still another possibility that has been suggested by the NCAA and is adhered to by some colleges is a college committee set up to interview agents and to advise athletes on specific agents. Some universities have banned certain agents from their campuses. This, however, hasn't stopped those agents from signing the athletes.

Coach Larry Smith, of the University of Southern California, has summarized the position of most coaches when he notes that the problem of dishonest and incompetent agents is "one of the most critical problems for both college and professional athletes. All would benefit from strong controls."

NCAA Standards

The NCAA can set standards for agents and for registration of agents. The problem is that such rules have no special force. The NCAA has no real enforcement powers and no subpoena power. However, the recent United States Supreme Court decision regarding University of Nevada at Las Vegas basketball coach Jerry Tarkanian has added some support to the possible regulatory powers of the NCAA. The decision indicates that the NCAA cannot be sued on constitutional grounds.

One possible solution would be to allow only agents certified by the NCAA to negotiate with and to sign contracts with athletes who are still on scholarship. The Court's decision, which found the NCAA to be a "private actor" when it represents the interests of its university members, may give it such power. It will now have wider authority over collegiate sports.

The scholarship contracts between the universities and the athletes could include provisions for civil, and possible criminal, penalties for athletes who negotiate or sign with a nonapproved agent.

State Regulations

The existing state regulations are too conflicting, confusing, and cumbersome. Because of the heavy financial bonds that are usually required, competent agents may not be able to work nationally. Their potential clients would then be reduced and the cost to the athletes would have to be higher—to cover the cost of doing business for the agent.

Perhaps the states could agree on a uniform code and allow for an agent registered in one state to be allowed to practice in all states. This, of course, would be far more expensive to administer than a program handled by the federal government or the professional athletes associations.

Federal Regulations

Most of the people involved believe that the most effective regulation would be done with federal legislation. Both civil and criminal penalties could be determined for both the athlete and the unethical agent. The registration fees of the agents could totally fund the program so that there would be no cost to the taxpayers.

Possible Solutions to Other Problems

A major problem is in discovering which agents and athletes are acting unethically. The dishonest athlete does not want to expose himself to possible legal actions, public ridicule, or even potential physical harm. For this reason it has been very difficult to get athletes to complain or testify.

Since it is generally known that the few agents who have been exposed and penalized are just the tip of the iceberg, effective enforcement of the rules and laws that govern the athlete-agent relationship requires more information.

Illegal Activities Reported by Players

In the confidential survey some of the honest agents suggested that the athletes keep the "gifts" and "loans" from the dishonest agents but then sign with an honest agent. If every athlete did that it might soon put the incompetents out of business.

Another suggestion has been to allow the athlete to become an informant and keep any money given during his college eligibility. The NCAA might even fund whatever additional money was proven to have been promised to the athlete. There is a recent precedent for this.

Hart Lee Dykes was granted immunity by the NCAA and was allowed to play his senior year at Oklahoma State after testifying to the NCAA. Dykes gained All-American honors in 1988 and played in the 1989 Hula and Shrine East-West games. His testimony was very influential in the investigations of illegal recruiting by Oklahoma, Oklahoma State, Illinois, and Texas A & M. All were penalized by the NCAA.

Two problems exist with the idea of immunity for athletes or sting operations. One is proving that the alleged loans, gifts, or payment of living expenses were given by the dishonest agents. A solution might be to use special surveillance methods. A second problem exists with the payment of additional money by the NCAA to the athlete. This would be over and above the scholarship money, used in lieu of the money that would have been given by the unethical agent.

These possibilities have to be weighed against the advantage of eliminating the unethical agents. It probably would not take many situations to greatly reduce the number of illegal offerings. But does the end justify the means?

Perhaps a better idea is to have the NCAA employ some outstanding high school seniors. These players could then report back to the NCAA about illegal recruiting practices and illegal agent offers. If 20 to 50 players were employed each year, the NCAA could get a great deal of information and perhaps reduce their own enforcement division costs while getting better information.

Conclusion

Something must be done to reduce the number of unethical agents and to protect the athletes from being exposed to the civil and criminal penalties that can occur when they sign early contracts. They should also be protected against having their money handled by incompetent and dishonest people.

Let us know about your suggestions for solutions. We would like to include them in the next edition.

APPENDIX A

NCAA Constitutional Provisions Relating to Student-Athletes

Article Three

Principles for the Conduct of Intercollegiate Athletics

Section 1. Principle of Amateurism and Student Participation. An amateur student-athlete is one who engages in a particular sport for the educational, physical, mental and social benefits derived therefrom and to whom participation in that sport is an avocation. *(Revised: 1/9/74)*

O.I. 1. A "student-athlete" is a student whose matriculation was solicited by a member of the athletics staff or other representative of athletics interests with a view toward the student's ultimate participation in the intercollegiate athletics program. Any other student becomes a "student-athlete" only when the student reports for an intercollegiate squad that is under the jurisdiction of the department of intercollegiate athletics as specified in O.I. 12. A student is not deemed a "student-athlete" solely because of prior participation in high school athletics.

(a) An individual shall not be eligible for participation in an intercollegiate sport if the individual: *(Revised: 1/10/79)* [Case Nos. 3 through 6]
  (1) Takes or has taken pay, or has accepted the promise of pay, in any form, for participation in that sport, including the promise of pay

when such pay is to be received following completion of the intercollegiate career; or [Case Nos. 7 through 15, 107]

(2) Has entered into an agreement of any kind to compete in professional athletics in that sport or to negotiate a professional contract in the sport; or [Case Nos. 16 through 20]

(3) Has directly or indirectly used athletic skill for pay in any form in that sport; however, an individual may: *(Revised: 1/9/74, 1/8/75, 1/13/78, 1/16/85)* [Case Nos. 7 through 9, 11 through 14, 21 through 26, 107, 219]

   (i) Accept or have accepted scholarships or educational grants-in-aid administered by an educational institution that do not conflict with the governing legislation of this Association;

   (ii) Receive compensation authorized by the United States Olympic Committee to cover financial loss occurring as a result of absence from employment to prepare for or participate in the Olympic Games, and [Case No. 22]

   (iii) Borrow against his or her future earnings potential from an established, accredited commercial lending institution exclusively for the purpose of purchasing insurance (with no cash surrender value) against a disabling injury that would prevent the individual from pursuing his or her chosen career, provided no third party (including a member institution's athletics department staff members or representatives of its athletics interests) is involved in arrangements for securing the loan. The student-athlete shall report any such transactions to the member institution and shall file copies of the loan documents and insurance policy with the member institution. *(Adopted: 1/16/85)* [Case No. 8]

   (iv) Utilize athletic ability to win a prize as a result of participation in a member institution's promotional activities, provided the receipt of the prize is consistent with the provisions of Bylaw 4-1 or official interpretations approved by the NCAA Council. *(Adopted: 1/13/88)*

O.I. 2. The term "pay" specifically includes, but is not limited to, receipt directly or indirectly of any salary, gratuity or comparable compensation; division or split of surplus; educational expenses not permitted by governing legislation of this Association, and excessive or improper expenses, awards and benefits. Competitive awards received by individuals prior to collegiate enrollment shall conform to the regulations of the amateur organization applicable to the event, except the receipt of cash for such participation shall not be permitted in any case. Expenses received from an outside amateur sports team or organization in excess of actual and necessary travel and meal expenses for practice and game competition shall be considered pay.

(b) Any individual who signs or who has ever signed a contract or commitment of any kind to play professional athletics in a sport, regardless of its legal enforceability or the consideration (if any) received; plays or has ever played on any professional athletics team in a sport, or receives or has ever received, directly or indirectly, a salary, reimbursement of expenses or any other form of financial assistance from a professional organization in a sport based upon athletic skill or participation, except as permitted by the governing legislation of this Association, no longer shall be eligible for intercollegiate athletics in that sport. (*Revised: 1/9/74, 1/18/75, 1/10/79*) [Case Nos. 1 through 6, 27 through 29]

(1) A student-athlete shall be eligible although, prior to enrollment in a collegiate institution, the student-athlete may have tried out at his or her own expense with a professional athletics team in a sport or received not more than one expense-paid visit from any one professional organization in a sport, provided such a visit did not exceed 48 hours and any payment or compensation in connection with the visit was not in excess of actual and necessary expenses. [Case No. 30]

(2) A student-athlete shall not try out with a professional athletics team in a sport during any part of the academic year (i.e., from the beginning of the fall term through completion of the spring term, including any intervening vacation period) while enrolled in a collegiate institution as a regular student in at least a minimum full-time academic load, unless the student-athlete has exhausted eligibility in his or her sport. The student-athlete may try out with a professional organization in a sport during the summer or during the academic year while not a full-time student, provided the student-athlete does not receive any form of expenses or other compensation from the professional organization. (*Revised: 1/10/79*) [Case No. 31]

(c) Any individual who contracts or who has ever contracted orally or in writing to be represented by an agent in the marketing of the individual's athletic ability or reputation in a sport no longer shall be eligible for intercollegiate athletics in that sport. An agency contract not specifically limited in writing to a particular sport or particular sports shall be deemed applicable to all sports. Securing advice from a lawyer concerning a proposed professional sports contract shall not be considered contracting for representation by an agent under this rule unless the lawyer also represents the student-athlete in negotiations for such a contract. A proposed contract also may be reviewed by an authorized institutional career counseling panel, which may meet with the student-athlete and representatives of professional teams. Any individual, agency or organization representing a prospective student-athlete for compensation in placing the prospect in a collegiate institution as a recipient of athletically related financial aid shall be considered an agent or organization marketing the athletic ability or reputation of the individual. (*Revised: 8/1/74, 1/17/76, 1/10/79, 1/14/86*) [Case Nos. 3, 4, 32 through 34]

(d) An individual may participate singly or as a member of a team against professional athletes; but if the individual participates or has ever participated on a team known to the individual or which reasonably should have been known to the individual to be a professional team in that sport, that individual no longer shall be eligible for intercollegiate athletics in that sport. (*Revised: 1/9/74, 1/10/79*) [Case Nos. 3, 6, 35 through 37]

O.I. 3. A professional team shall be any organized team that is a member of a recognized professional sports organization, that is directly supported or sponsored by a professional team or professional sports organization, that is a member of a playing league that is directly supported or sponsored by a professional team or professional sports organization, or on which there is an athlete receiving directly or indirectly payment of any kind from a professional team or professional sports organization for the athlete's participation. [Case No. 35]

O.I. 4. A noncollegiate amateur team or playing league that receives financial support from a national amateur sports administrative organization or an administrative equivalent, either of which receives developmental funds from a professional team or professional sports organization, shall not be considered a professional team or league.

O.I. 5. An individual may compete on tennis or golf teams with persons who are competing for cash or a comparable prize, provided the individual does not receive payment of any kind for such participation.

(e) Subsequent to becoming a student-athlete (per O.I. 1), an individual shall not be eligible for participation in intercollegiate athletics if the individual accepts any remuneration for or permits the use of his or her name or picture to directly advertise, recommend or promote the sale or use of a commercial product or service of any kind or receives remuneration for endorsing a commercial product or service through the individual's use of such product or service. (*Revised: 8/1/72, 1/9/74*) [Case Nos. 38 through 48, 219]

APPENDIX B-1

Bylaw, Article 12: Amateurism

12.01 General Principles

12.01.1 Eligibility for Intercollegiate Athletics. Only an amateur student-athlete is eligible for intercollegiate athletics participation in a particular sport. C 3-1-(a)

12.01.2 Clear Line of Demarcation. Member institutions' athletics programs are designed to be an integral part of the educational program and the student-athlete is considered an integral part of the student body, thus maintaining a clear line of demarcation between college athletics and professional sports. C 2-2-(a)

12.01.3 "Individual" vs. "Student-Athlete." NCAA amateur status may be lost as a result of activities prior to enrollment in college. If NCAA rules specify that an "individual" may or may not participate in certain activities, this term refers to a person prior to and subsequent to enrollment in a member institution. If NCAA rules specify a "student-athlete," the legislation applies only to that person's activities subsequent to enrollment. CB 3

12.01.4 Permissible Grant-in-Aid. A grant-in-aid administered by an educational institution is not considered to be pay or the promise of pay for athletics skill, provided it does not exceed the financial aid limitations set by the Association's membership. C 3-1-(a)-(3), C 3-1-(a)-(3)-(1)

12.02 Definitions and Applications

12.02.1 Amateur Student-Athlete. An amateur student-athlete is one who engages in a particular sport for the educational, physical, mental and social benefits derived therefrom and for whom participation in that sport is an avocation. C 3-1

12.02.2 Individual. An individual, for purposes of this bylaw, is any person of any age without reference to enrollment in an educational institution or status as a student-athlete. CB 3

12.02.3 Pay. Pay is the receipt of funds, awards, or benefits not permitted by the governing legislation of the Association for participation in athletics. C 3-1-(g)

12.02.4 Professional Athlete. A professional athlete is one who receives any kind of payment, directly or indirectly, for athletics participation except as permitted by the governing legislation of the Association. OI 3

12.02.5 Professional Athletics Team. A professional team is any organized team that:

(a) Is a member of a recognized professional sports organization;
(b) Is directly supported or sponsored by a professional team or professional sports organization;
(c) Is a member of a playing league that is directly supported or sponsored by a professional team or professional sports organization; or
(d) Has an athlete receiving for his or her participation any kind of payment, directly or indirectly, from a professional team or professional sports organization. OI 3

12.02.6 Student-Athlete. A student-athlete is a student whose enrollment was solicited by a member of the athletics staff or other representative of athletics interests with a view toward the student's ultimate participation in the intercollegiate athletics program. Any other student becomes a student-athlete only when the student reports for an intercollegiate squad that is under the jurisdiction of the athletics department, as specified in 3.2.4.4. A student is not deemed a student-athlete solely on the basis of prior high school athletics participation. OI 1

12.1 General Regulations

An individual must comply with the following to retain amateur status. (See Bylaw 14 regarding the eligibility appeal process.) (New)

12.1.1 Amateur Status. An individual loses amateur status and thus shall not be eligible for intercollegiate competition in a particular sport if the individual:

(a) Uses his or her athletics skill (directly or indirectly) for pay in any form in that sport; C 3-1-(a)-(3)
(b) Accepts a promise of pay even if such pay is to be received following completion of intercollegiate athletics participation; C 3-1-(a)-(1)
(c) Signs a contract or commitment of any kind to play professional athletics, regardless of its legal enforceability or any consideration received; C 3-1-(b)
(d) Receives, directly or indirectly, a salary, reimbursement of expenses or any other form of financial assistance from a professional sports organization based upon athletics skill or participation, except as permitted by NCAA rules and regulations; C 3-1-(b)
(e) Competes on any professional athletics team and knows (or had reason to know) that the team is a professional athletics team (per 12.0.2.5), even if no pay or remuneration for expenses was received, or C 3-1-(b), C 3-1-(d)
(f) Enters into a professional draft or an agreement with an agent or other entity to negotiate a professional contract. C 3-1-(a)-(2), CB 17, CB 19, CB 20

12.1.1.1 Use of Overall Athletics Skill—Effect on Eligibility. Participation for pay in competition that involves the use of overall athletics skill (e.g., "superstars" competition) constitutes a violation of the Association's amateur-status regulations; therefore, an individual participating for pay in such competition is ineligible for intercollegiate competition in all sports. CB 4, C 3-1-(a)-(3)

12.1.1.2 Road Racing. "Road racing" is essentially the same as cross country or track competition and cannot be separated effectively from those sports for purposes of Bylaw 12. Therefore, a student-athlete who accepts pay in any form for participation in such a race is ineligible for intercollegiate cross country or track competition. CB 5

12.1.2 Forms of Pay. An individual loses amateur status through receipt of "pay," which includes, but is not limited to, the following practices: C 3-1-(g)

(a) Educational expenses not permitted by the governing legislation of this Association (see Bylaw 15 regarding permissible financial aid to enrolled student-athletes); OI 2, CB 13
(b) Any direct or indirect salary, gratuity or comparable compensation; OI 2
(c) Any division or split of surplus (bonuses, game receipts, etc.); OI 2
(d) Excessive or improper expenses, awards and benefits (see Bylaw 16 regarding permissible awards, benefits and expenses to enrolled student-athletes); OI 2
(e) Expenses received from an outside amateur sports team or organization in excess of actual and necessary travel, room and board expenses for practice and game competition; OI 2
(f) Actual and necessary expenses or any other form of compensation to participate in athletics competition (while not representing an educational institution) from a sponsor other than an individual upon whom the athlete is naturally or legally dependent or the nonprofessional organization that is sponsoring the competition; CB 7
(g) Payment to individual team members or individual competitors for unspecified or unitemized expenses beyond actual and necessary travel, room and board expenses for practice and competition; C 3-1-(g)-(2), C 3-1-(g)-(2)-(i)
(h) Expenses incurred or awards received by an individual that are prohibited by the rules governing an amateur, noncollegiate event in which the individual participates; C 3-1-(g)-(2)-(ii), OI 2
(i) Any payment, including actual and necessary expenses, conditioned on the individual's or team's place finish or performance or given on an incentive basis, or receipt of expenses in excess of the same reasonable amount for permissible expenses given to all individuals or team members involved in the competition; CB 11, CB 10
(j) Educational expenses provided to an individual by an outside sports team or organization that are based in any degree upon the recipient's athletics ability, even if the funds are given to the institution to administer to the recipient; CB 12
(k) Cash, or the equivalent thereof (e.g., trust fund), as an award for participation in competition at any time, even if such an award is permitted under the rules governing an amateur, noncollegiate event

in which the individual is participating. An award or a cash prize that an individual could not receive under NCAA legislation may not be forwarded in the individual's name to a different individual or agency; CB 107, OI 2, CB 9, LIC 87-27.4

(l) Preferential treatment, benefits or services (e.g., loans with deferred pay-back) because of the individual's athletic's reputation or skill or pay-back potential as a professional athlete, unless such treatment, benefits or services are specifically permitted under NCAA legislation, and C 3-1-(a)-(3)-(iii), CB 8

(m) Receipt of a prize for participation (involving the utilization of athletics ability) in a member institution's promotional activity that is inconsistent with the provisions of 12.5 or official interpretations approved by the NCAA Council. C 3-1-(a)-(3)-(iv)

12.1.2.1 Exception for insurance against Disabling Injury. An individual may borrow against his or her future earnings potential from an established, accredited commercial lending institution exclusively for the purpose of purchasing insurance (with no cash surrender value) against a disabling injury that would prevent the individual from pursuing a chosen career, provided a third party (including a member institution's athletics department staff members or representatives of its athletics interests) is not involved in arrangements for securing the loan. The student-athlete shall report all such transactions and shall file copies of the loan documents and insurance policy with the member institution. C 3-1-(a)-(3)-(iii)

12.1.2.2 Institutional Fund-Raising Activities Involving the Athletics Ability of Student-Athletes. Institutional fund-raising activities that involve the use of athletics ability by student-athletes to obtain funds (e.g., "win-a-thons") are permitted only if:

(a) The money is contributed directly to the institution by the donor, and

(b) The student-athletes receive no compensation or prizes for their participation. LA 86-6

12.1.3 Professionalism. An individual is not eligible for participation in an intercollegiate sport if that individual ever has been a professional in that sport. An individual becomes a professional if he or she:

(a) Signs a contract or commitment of any kind to participate in professional athletics in that sport, regardless of its legal enforceability or any consideration received;

(b) Participates on a team and knows (or had reason to know) that the team is a professional athletics team (per 12.02.5) in that sport; or

(c) Receives, directly or indirectly, a salary, reimbursement of expenses or any other form of financial assistance from a professional organization in that sport based upon athletics skill or participation, except as permitted by the Association's legislation. C 3-1-(b), C 3-1-(d)

12.1.4 Amateur Status if Professional in Another Sport. A professional athlete in one sport may represent a member institution in a different sport. However, the student-athlete cannot receive institutional financial assistance in the second sport unless the student-athlete:

(a) Is no longer involved in professional athletics;
(b) Is not receiving any remuneration from a professional sports organization; and
(c) Has no active contractual relationship with any professional athletics team. However, an individual may remain bound by an option clause in a professional sports contract that requires assignment to a particular team if the student-athlete's professional career is resumed. CB 129

12.1.4.1 Professional at Later Date. If the individual later becomes involved in professional athletics while still a student-athlete with remaining eligibility, the individual would be considered to have violated the principles of ethical conduct per Bylaw 10, thus rendering the individual ineligible for intercollegiate competition. CB 129

12.2 Involvement with Professional Teams

12.2.1 Tryouts.

12.2.1.1 Tryout Prior to Enrollment. A student-athlete remains eligible in a sport even though, prior to enrollment in a collegiate institution, the student-athlete may have tried out with a professional athletics team in a sport or received not more than one expense-paid visit from any one professional organization in a sport, provided such a visit did not exceed 48 hours and any payment or compensation in connection with the visit was not in excess of actual and necessary expenses. A self-financed tryout may be for any length of time. C 3-1-(b)-(1), CB 30

12.2.1.2 Tryout after Enrollment. A student-athlete shall not try out with a professional athletics team in a sport during any part of the academic year (i.e., from the beginning of the fall term through completion of the spring term, including any intervening vacation period) while enrolled in a collegiate institution as a regular student in at least a minimum full-time academic load, unless the student-athlete has exhausted eligibility in that sport. The student-athlete may try out with a professional organization in a sport during the summer or during the academic year while not a full-time student, provided the student-athlete does not receive any form of expenses or other compensation from the professional organization. C 3-1-(b)-(2)

12.2.1.3 Outside Competition Prohibited. During a tryout, an individual may not take part in any outside competition (games or scrimmages) as a representative of a professional team. C 3-1-(d)

12.2.1.4 Professional Team Representative at College Practice. A tryout with a professional team is not considered to have occurred when a representative of a professional football team visits a member institution during the academic year and evaluates a student-athlete while the institution is conducting a regular practice session that includes physical activities (e.g., speed trials, agility tests, strength tests), provided these activities are normally a part of regular practice sessions and take place during such sessions. CB 31

12.2.2 Practice without Competition. An individual may participate in practice sessions conducted by a professional team, provided such participation meets the requirements of NCAA legislation governing tryouts with professional athletics teams (see 12.2.1) and the individual does not:

(a) Receive any compensation for participation in the practice sessions,
(b) Enter into any contract or agreement with a professional team or sports organization, or
(c) Take part in any outside competition (games or scrimmages) as a representative of a professional team. CB 6

12.2.2.1 Prohibited Involvement of Institution's Coach. An institution's coaching staff member may not arrange for or direct student-athletes' participation in football or basketball practice sessions conducted by a professional team. CB 6

12.2.3 Competition.

12.2.3.1 Competition against Professionals. An individual may participate singly or as a member of an amateur team against professional athletes. C 3-1-(d)

12.2.3.2 Competition with Professionals. An individual shall not be eligible for intercollegiate athletics in a sport if the individual ever participated on a team and knew (or had reason to know) that the team was a professional team (per 12.02.5) in that sport. However, an individual may compete on tennis or golf teams with persons who are competing for cash or a comparable prize, provided the individual does not receive payment of any kind for such participation. C 3-1-(d), OI 5

12.2.3.2.1 Professional Player as Team Member. An individual may participate with a professional on a team, provided the professional is not being paid by a professional team or league to play as a member of that team (e.g., summer basketball leagues with teams composed of both professional and amateur athletes). OI 3, LA 86-18

12.2.3.2.2 Professional Coach or Referee. Participation on a team that includes a professional coach or referee does not cause the team to be classified as a professional team. CB 35

12.2.3.2.3 Amateur/Professional Leagues. An individual may participate as a member of an amateur team in a league in which one or more teams are professional, provided the league is not a member of a recognized professional sports organization or is not directly supported or sponsored by a professional sports team or organization. CB 36, OI 3

12.2.3.2.4 Major Junior A Ice Hockey. Ice hockey teams in the United States and Canada, classified by the Canadian Amateur Hockey Association as major junior A teams, are considered professional teams under NCAA legislation. Participation by any individual on a major junior A hockey team subsequent to June 26, 1980, shall be considered prima facie evidence that the individual has participated on a team that the individual knew (or had reason to know) was a professional team and shall render the participant ineligible for intercollegiate athletics in ice hockey. CB 37

12.2.3.2.4.1 Limitation on Restoration of Eligibility. An individual who has been involved in such participation is entitled to appeal for restoration of eligibility under the provisions of 14.14; however, such individual shall be denied at least the first year of intercollegiate athletics competition in the sport of ice hockey at the certifying institution and shall be charged with the loss of at least one season of eligibility in the sport of ice hockey. CB 37 (*Revised: 1/11/89*)

12.2.3.3 Competition in Professional All-Star Contest. A student-athlete who agrees to participate in a professional (players to be paid) all-star game becomes ineligible to compete in any intercollegiate contest that occurs subsequent to that agreement. Thus, a senior entering into such an agreement immediately following the last regular-season intercollegiate contest would not be eligible to compete in a bowl game, an NCAA championship or any other certified postseason collegiate contest. CB 27

12.2.4 Draft.

12.2.4.1 Inquiry. An individual may inquire about eligibility for a professional-league player draft without affecting his or her amateur status. CB 16

12.2.4.2 Draft List. An individual loses amateur status in a particular sport when the individual asks to be placed on the draft list or supplemental draft list of a professional league in that sport, even though: CB 17, LIC 88-124

(a) The individual asks that his or her name be withdrawn from the draft list prior to the actual draft, CB 18

(b) The individual's name remains on the list but he or she is not drafted, or CB 19

(c) The individual is drafted but does not sign an agreement with any professional athletics team. CB 20

12.2.5 Contracts and Compensation.

12.2.5.1 General Rule. An individual shall be ineligible for participation in an intercollegiate sport if he or she has entered into any kind of agreement to compete in professional athletics or to negotiate a professional contract in that sport, regardless of the legal enforceability of that agreement. C 3-1-(a)-(2), C 3-1-(b)

12.2.5.1.1 Nonbinding Agreements. An individual who signs a contract or commitment that does not become binding until the professional organization's representative or agent also signs the document is ineligible, even if the contract remains unsigned by the other parties until after the student-athlete's eligibility is exhausted. CB 28

12.3 Use of Agents

12.3.1 General Rule. An individual shall be ineligible for participation in an intercollegiate sport if he or she ever has agreed (orally or in writing) to be represented by an agent for the purpose of marketing his or her athletics ability or reputation in that sport. Further, an agency contract not specifically limited in writing to a sport or particular sports shall be deemed applicable to all sports and the individual shall be ineligible to participate in any sport. C 3-1-(c)

12.3.1.1 Representation for Future Negotiations. An individual shall be ineligible per 12.3.1 if he or she enters into a verbal or written agreement with an agent for representation in future professional sports negotiations that are to take place after the individual has completed his or her eligibility in that sport. CB 32

12.3.1.2 Benefits from Prospective Agents. An individual shall be ineligible per 12.3.1 if he or she (or his or her relatives or friends) accepts transportation or other benefits from any person who wishes to represent the individual in the marketing of his or her athletic ability. The receipt of such expenses constitutes compensation based on athletic skill and is an extra benefit not available to the student body in general. CB 24, LIC 87-3.8

12.3.2 Legal Counsel. Securing advice from a lawyer concerning a proposed professional sports contract shall not be considered contracting for representation by an agent under this rule, unless the lawyer also represents the student-athlete in negotiations for such a contract. C 3-1-(c)

12.3.2.1 Presence of a Lawyer at Negotiations. A lawyer may not be present during discussions of a contract offer with a professional organization or have any direct contact (i.e., in person, by telephone or by mail) with a professional sports organization on behalf of the student-athlete. A lawyer's presence during such discussions is considered representation by an agent. CB 33

12.3.3 Athletic Scholarship Agent. Any individual, agency, or organization that represents a prospective student-athlete for compensation in placing the prospect in a collegiate institution as a recipient of institutional financial aid shall be considered an agent or organization marketing the individual's athletic ability or reputation. C 3-1-(c)

12.3.3.1 Talent Evaluation Services and Agents. A prospect may allow a scouting service or agent to distribute personal information (e.g., high school academic and athletics records, physical statistics) to member institutions without jeopardizing his or her eligibility, provided the fee paid to such an agent is not based on placing the prospect in a collegiate institution as a recipient of institutional financial aid. CB 34

12.3.4 Career Counseling Panel. It is permissible for an authorized institutional career counseling panel to:

(a) Advise a student-athlete about a future professional career,
(b) Review a proposed professional sports contract, and
(c) Meet with the student-athlete and representatives of professional teams. C 3-1-(c), C 3-1-(h)-(4)-(vi)

12.3.4.1 Appointment by Chief Executive Officer. This panel shall consist of at least three persons appointed by the institution's chief executive officer (or his or her designated representative from outside the athletics department). C 3-1-(h)-(4)-(vi)

12.3.4.2 Composition. No more than one panel member may be an athletics department staff member. All other panel members must be selected by the institution from among its full-time employees employed outside the athletics department. All panel members shall be identified to the NCAA national office. C 3-1-(h)-(4)-(vi)

APPENDIX B-2

Bylaw Article 16.12

16.12 Benefits, Gifts, and Services

16.12.1 Permissible

16.12.1.1 General Rule. Receipt of a benefit (including otherwise prohibited extra benefits per 16.12.2) by student-athletes, their relatives or friends is not a violation of NCAA rules if it is demonstrated that the same benefit is generally available to the institution's students and their relatives or friends. C 3-1-(g)-(5)

16.12.1.2 Disabling-Injury Insurance. A student-athlete may borrow against his or her future earnings potential from an established, accredited commercial lending institution, exclusively for the purpose of purchasing insurance (with no cash surrender value) against a disabling injury that would prevent the individual from pursuing his or her chosen career, provided a third party (including a member institution's athletics department staff members or representatives of its athletics interests) is not involved in arrangements for securing the loan. The student-athlete shall report any such transactions to the member institution and shall file copies of the loan documents and insurance policy with the member institution. C 3-1-(a)-(3)-(iii)

16.12.1.3 Promotional Activity Prizes. A student-athlete from a member institution, selected through a random drawing open to the general public or the student body, may receive a prize as part of a promotional activity conducted by a member institution or held on a member institution's campus only as specified in 16.12.1.3.1. C 3-1-(a)-(3)-(iv), C 3-1-(g)-(5)-(ix), B 4-1-(g), CB 45

16.12.1.3.1 Athletics Ability. The utilization of athletics ability (e.g., making a half-court basketball shot) to win such a prize is governed by division regulations as follows:

(a) Divisions I and II—Not permitted, and CB 45

(b) Division III—Permitted. B 4-1-(g)

16.12.1.4 Occasional Meals. A student-athlete may receive an occasional family home meal from an institutional staff member or representative of athletics interests. The meal must be provided in an individual's home and must be restricted to infrequent and special occasions (e.g., Thanksgiving, Christmas). LA 87-7

16.12.1.5 Retention of Athletics Apparel. A student-athlete may retain athletics apparel items (not equipment) at the end of the individual's collegiate participation. Council (1/4/87)

16.12.1.6 Summer Use of Athletics Equipment. A student-athlete may retain and use institutional athletics equipment (per the institution's normal equipment policy) during a summer vacation period. LIC 87-3.10

16.12.2 Nonpermissible

16.12.2.1 General Rule. The student-athlete shall not receive any extra benefit. The term "extra benefit" refers to any special arrangement by an institutional employee or representative of the institution's athletics interests to provide the student-athlete or his or her relatives or friends with a benefit not expressly authorized by NCAA legislation. C 3-1-(g)-(5)

16.12.2.2 Discounts and Credits. A student-athlete may not receive a special discount, payment arrangement, or credit on a purchase (e.g., airline ticket, clothing) or a service (e.g., laundry, dry cleaning) from an institutional employee or a representative of its athletics interests. C 3-1-(g)-(5)-(i)

16.12.2.2.1 Free or Reduced-Cost Services. An athletics representative may not provide a student-athlete with professional services (for which a fee normally would be charged) without charge or at a reduced cost except as permitted elsewhere in this bylaw. Professional services provided at less than the normal rate or at no expense to a student-athlete are considered an extra benefit unless they are available on the same basis to the general student body. CB 64

16.12.2.2.2 Telephones and Credit Cards. It is not permissible to allow a student-athlete to use a telephone or credit card for personal reasons without charge or at a reduced cost. CB 80

16.12.2.2.3 Entertainment Services. A student-athlete may not receive services (e.g., movie tickets, dinners, use of car) from commercial agencies (e.g., movie theaters, restaurants, car dealers) without charge or at reduced rates, or free or reduced-cost admission to professional athletics contests from professional sports organizations, unless such services also are available to the student body in general. CB 84, CB 86

16.12.2.3 Other Prohibited Benefits. An institutional employee or representative of the institution's athletics interests may not provide a student-athlete with extra benefits or services, including, but not limited to: C 3-1-(g)-(5)

(a) A loan of money, C 3-1-(g)-(5)-(ii)
(b) A guarantee of bond, C 3-1-(g)-(5)-(iii)
(c) The use of an automobile, or C 3-1-(g)-(5)-(iv)
(d) Signing or cosigning a note with an outside agency to arrange a loan. C 3-1-(g)-(5)-(vii)

16.12.2.4 Preferential Treatment. A student-athlete may not receive preferential treatment, benefits, or services (e.g., loans on a deferred pay-back basis) for his or her athletics reputation or skill or pay-back potential as a future professional athlete (see 16.12.1.2 for disabling-injury insurance exception). CB 8

16.12.2.5 Camp Concession. It is not permissible for a member institution or a member of its athletics department staff conducting a sports camp to permit a student-athlete (enrolled in the institution) to operate, at the student-athlete's own expense, a concession selling items related to or associated with the camp to campers or others in attendance. CB 67

16.12.2.6 Athletics Equipment. A student-athlete may not accept athletics equipment, supplies, or clothing (e.g., tennis racquets, golf clubs, hockey sticks, balls, shirts) from a manufacturer or commercial enterprise. Such items may be provided to the student-athlete's institution, to be utilized by the institution's team in accordance with accepted practices, for issuance and retrieval of athletics equipment. CB 68

16.12.2.7 Sponsor Families. A member institution shall not permit individuals outside the institution to serve as "sponsors" or "families" for student-athletes who are enrolled in the institution unless such a sponsorship program exists to provide the same benefits and support services to all students at the institution. CB 69

16.12.2.8 Civic-Group Gifts. A member institution shall not permit a civic group to provide a student-athlete a trip to a postseason football game or to pay summer-camp expenses for a student-athlete. CB 81

APPENDIX C

NCAA Cases Regarding Student-Athlete Eligibility

No. 3—Participation for Pay

Situation: Prior to enrollment in a collegiate institution, a student-athlete engages in one or more activities that are contrary to NCAA professional rulings described in Constitution 3-1-(a), 3-1-(b), 3-1-(c) and 3-1-(d) (e.g., signs a professional contract, plays athletics for pay, enters into an agreement with an agent, receives excessive expenses for reporting to or visiting a professional team, plays on a professional team). (6A)

Question: Does one or more of these occurrences prior to college enrollment affect the student-athlete's eligibility when the student-athlete enrolls in a NCAA member institution?

Answer: Yes. The provisions of these rules apply to a person at any time. [C-3-1-(a), C 3-1-(b), C 3-1-(c) and C 3-1-(d)]

No. 7—Student-Athlete Sponsorship

Situation: An individual (e.g., tennis player or golfer), who is not representing an educational institution, participates in athletics competition. (387)

Question: Is it permissible for a sponsor, other than an individual upon whom the athlete is naturally or legally dependent or the nonprofessional organization that is sponsoring the competition in question, to provide ac-

tual and necessary expenses or any other form of compensation to participate in the competition?

Answer: No. [C 3-1-(a)-(1), C 3-1-(a)-(3), C 3-1-(g)-(2) and C 3-4-(a)]

No. 8—Professional Ruling—Extra Benefits

Situation: An individual receives preferential treatment, benefits, or services (e.g., loans with deferred pay-back basis) because of the individual's athletics reputation or skill or pay-back potential as a future professional athlete. (343)

Question: Does entering into such an arrangement or receiving such benefits or services render the individual ineligible under the Association's professional rulings?

Answer: Yes, except as specifically permitted under the provisions of Constitution 3-1-(a)-(3)-(iii). [C 3-1-(a)-(1), C 3-1-(a)-(3) and C 3-1-(g)-(5)]

No. 16—Professional Draft

Situation: An individual with eligibility remaining is interested in being considered eligible for a professional league's player draft. (99)

Question: Does an individual become a professional by inquiring whether the individual is eligible for the draft?

Answer: No. Merely making inquiry regarding eligibility does not professionalize the student-athlete for purposes of intercollegiate competition. [C 3-1-(a)-(2)]

No. 17—Professional Draft

Situation: An individual with eligibility remaining asks to be placed on the draft list of a professional sports league. (100)

Question: Does such action professionalize the individual in that sport in accordance with NCAA rules?

Answer: Yes. [C 3-1-(a)-(2)]

No. 18—Professional Draft

Situation: An individual with eligibility remaining agrees to be placed on the draft list of a professional league, then asks to be withdrawn prior to the actual draft. (101)

Question: Since the individual asked to be withdrawn from the list prior to the actual draft, does the individual remain eligible for intercollegiate athletics?

Answer: No. [C 3-1-(a)-(2)]

No. 19—Professional Draft

Situation: An individual with eligibility remaining asks to be placed on a professional league's draft list and is on the list at the time of the draft, but the individual is not drafted. (102)

Question: Is the individual a professional?

Answer: Yes. The individual became a professional by asking to be placed on the draft list (i.e., entering into an agreement to negotiate). [C 3-1-(a)-(2)]

No. 20—Professional Draft

Situation: An individual with eligibility remaining asks to be placed on a professional league's draft list. The individual is subsequently drafted but does not sign with any team. (103)

Question: Has the individual become professionalized?

Answer: Yes. The fact that the individual actually did not sign an agreement with a professional team does not negate the fact that the individual became ineligible by entering into an agreement to negotiate a professional contract. [C 3-1-(a)-(2)]

No. 24—Expenses from Agents

Situation: An individual with eligibility remaining in the individual's sport is offered transportation or other expenses by an agent who wishes to represent the individual in the marketing of the individual's athletic ability. (555)

Question: May the individual accept such expenses?

Answer: No. The receipt of such expenses would constitute compensation based on athletic skills, which is not permissible under NCAA legislation, as well as an extra benefit not available to the student body in general. [C 3-1-(a)-(3) and C 3-1-(g)-(5)]

No. 28—Signing Professional Agreement

Situation: An individual signs a contract or commitment to participate in professional athletics. This commitment does not become binding until the representative or agent of the professional organization also signs the document. (267)

Question: Does such signing by the individual, which does not result in a binding commitment, jeopardize the individual's eligibility under the Association's professional rulings?

Answer: Yes. Any individual who signs or has ever signed a contract or commitment of any kind to play professional athletics in a sport, regardless of its legal enforceability, no longer shall be eligible for intercollegiate athletics in that sport. [C 3-1-(b)]

No. 32—Professional Negotiations

Situation: An individual desires to enter into an agreement with an agent for representation in future professional negotiations in a sport that is to take place after the individual has completed eligibility in that sport. This agreement may take either a verbal or written form.

Question: May the individual agree to be represented by an agent without jeopardizing the individual's eligibility for the intercollegiate sport when the negotiations are to take place after completion of the individual's eligibility?

Answer: No. An individual who agrees or has ever agreed to be represented by an agent or an organization in the marketing of athletic ability or athletics reputation no longer shall be eligible for the intercollegiate sport. [C 3-1-(c)]

No. 33—Professional Sports Contract Advice

Situation: In accordance with Constitution 3-1-(c), a student-athlete may secure advice from a lawyer concerning a proposed professional sports contract provided the lawyer does not represent the student-athlete in negotiations for such a contract. (616)

Question: May the lawyer be present during discussions of a contract offer with the professional organization or have any direct contact (i.e., in person, by telephone or by mail) with the professional organization on behalf of the student-athlete without jeopardizing the student's eligibility for the intercollegiate sport?

Answer: No. The lawyer's presence during such discussion of a contract offer or contact with the professional organization on behalf of the student-athlete shall be considered representation of the student-athlete in negotiations for a professional contract and shall render the student-athlete ineligible for intercollegiate athletics in the involved sport. [C 3-1-(c)]

No. 34—High School Scouting Services and Agents

Situation: A prospective student-athlete agrees to be represented by a scouting service or agent for the distribution of personal information (e.g., high school academic and athletics records, physical statistics) to NCAA member institutions. (105)

Question: Does entering into such an agreement with a scouting service or agent jeopardize the prospect's eligibility for intercollegiate athletics at an NCAA member institution?

Answer: No. Such an agreement does not constitute "marketing" of the student's athletic ability unless the agent is compensated for placing the prospect in a collegiate institution as a recipient of athletically related financial aid. [C 3-1-(c)]

No. 64—Extra Benefit—Professional Services

Situation: A student-athlete receives professional services (for which a fee normally would be charged) for personal reasons from a representative of an institution's athletics interests. (249)

Question: Is it permissible for the athletics representative to provide such services free or at a reduced cost?

Answer: No. Professional services provided at less than normal or no expense to a student-athlete are considered an extra benefit unless such benefits are available to the student body in general. [C 3-1-(g)-(5)]

APPENDIX D

Code of Ethics for the Association of Representatives of Professional Athletes (ARPA)

Canon One

A Representative shall maintain the highest degree of integrity and competence in representing the professional athlete.

Rule 1-101 Representing Clients with Competence and Integrity

(A) A Representative shall not:
  (1) Violate a rule of conduct of this Code,
  (2) Use another to circumvent a rule of this Code,
  (3) Engage in illegal conduct involving a felony or conduct involving moral turpitude,
  (4) Engage in conduct involving dishonesty, fraud, deceit, or misrepresentation,
  (5) Engage in conduct prejudicial to the reasonable conduct of professional athletics,
  (6) Engage in conduct which adversely reflects on his fitness.

Rule 1-102 Information Regarding a Violation of This Code

(A) A Representative possessing information which is unprivileged as a matter of law and not protected by Rule 4-101 of this Code concerning a violation of Rule 1-101 shall report such information to the Committee on Discipline of the Association of Representatives of Professional Athletes immediately.

(B) A Representative shall be available to testify or produce a statement under oath as to the nature, source and details of the information described in Rule 1-102 (A).

Rule 1-103 Refusing to Accept a Client

(A) A Representative shall refrain from accepting the representation of a professional athlete when:
  (1) The Representative does not possess the competence through training by education or experience in a particular area.
  (2) The Representative's representation of the athlete will create differing or unresolvable conflict of interest with an existing client or with an existing financial enterprise.
  (3) The Representative has differing interests with those of his prospective client.

(B) A Representative must disclose in writing in advance of his representation of a professional athlete the nature and degree of his involvement in any matter in which he is recommending, suggesting, or advising that the athlete invest.

Rule 1-104 General

(A) A Representative shall not knowingly give aide to or cooperate in any way with another in conduct which would violate this Code.

(B) A Representative shall act in the best interests of the professional athlete, bearing in mind the high degree of trust and responsibility reposed in him as fiduciary.

(C) A Representative shall become familiar with the Collective Bargaining Agreement, Standard of Uniform Players Contract, Constitution, By-laws and League Rules of the League and such other relevant documents affecting wages, hours and working conditions of the players in the sport or sports in which he represents professional athletes.

Canon Two

A Representative shall be dignified in the conduct of his profession.

Rule 2-101 Representative's Letterhead, Stationery, etc.

(A) A Representative shall not compensate or give anything of value to representatives of the print, video or audio media or other communication media in return for professional publicity.

(B) The professional letterhead, business or calling card, stationery, announcements, office signs of a representative and his firm or organization shall be dignified and may:
  (1) List the representative's name, firm or organization name, firm members and their position,
  (2) List the address of the firm's office or offices, phone number, telex and other such information as may aid the professional athlete in locating the representative,
  (3) Indicate his membership in ARPA.

(C) A Representative in the operation of his firm may practice under a trade name, partnership, corporation, or professional association.

(D) The letterhead of the representative shall indicate the name or names of representatives associated with the firm. If the degree of participation by a representative in the firm is less than that of a partner or manager, the nature of such association shall be indicated on the firm's stationery.

Rule 2-102 A Representative Engaged in More Than One Profession or Business

(A) A Representative who is engaged both in representation of professional athletes and simultaneously in another profession or business shall clearly distinguish those businesses or professions on his letterhead, office sign, professional card, and other public communication.

(B) A Representative, who in addition to his traditional role as a representative, offers to provide services as an investment and/or financial advisor, counselor or director to a professional athlete or in any way assert or maintain control and/or management of the financial affairs of a professional athlete, whether for compensation or not, must be qualified to do so based upon training or experience.

(C) A Representative who assumes the role outlined in Section B of this Rule, shall fully disclose that role in his contract with the professional athlete he represents. Such contract shall provide at least a statement of the services to be provided in connection with investment counseling, the limitations of such services, if any, and the fees to be charged for such services.

(D) A Representative may use or permit the use of, in connection with his name, any earned degree or title.

Rule 2-103 Recommending Employment of the Representative

(A) A Representative shall not compensate in any way or give anything of value or promise to compensate a professional or amateur athlete to recommend or secure the representative's employment in any capacity.

(B) A Representative shall not compensate or give anything of value to any individual as a reward for recommending the representative's employment or for referring an athlete to the representative; except that a representative may pay the customary costs and charges in connection with a Professional Association and with ARPA.

(C) A Representative may receive without the payment of compensation, other than dues, referrals from appropriate referring agencies.

(D) A Representative may employ for compensation, with the consent of his client another representative or other professional to assist him in fulfilling his duties and obligations to a professional athlete he represents.

Rule 2-104 Fees for Service

(A) A Representative shall disclose, in advance of any representation agreement and in writing, the nature of his fees and the services to be performed for the fee.

(B) A Representative shall not enter into an agreement for, charge, or collect an illegal or clearly excessive fee.

(C) A Representative fee is clearly excessive when, after a review of the facts, an individual within the industry of reasonable prudence would be left with the firm conviction that the fee is in excess of a reasonable fee for the work performed.

(D) Among the factors relevant in determining whether a fee is reasonable are:

(1) The time, labor, expenses involved,
(2) The degree of expertise required and the level of expertise of the representative,
(3) The usual and customary charge in the industry for the services performed,
(4) The impact of the services to be performed on the workload of the representative,
(5) The relationship between the fee and the length of the athlete's contract.

(E) In determining his fee, the Representative shall consider the relationship between the fee and foreseeable length of the athlete's employment with the athletic team and shall make every reasonable effort not to inflict serious hardship on the athlete.

(F) A Representative may employ one of the following methods in establishing his fee;

(1) Fixed fee,
(2) Percentage fee,
(3) Contingent fee.

(G) A Representative shall never solicit nor accept any compensation for services rendered in connection with any other services to a professional athlete from a professional athletic team, club or club representative either directly or indirectly.
  (1) Prior disclosure of such compensation shall not result in a waiver of the prohibition set forth in 2-104 (G).
  (2) The prohibition set forth in 2-104 (G) may not be waived by prior agreement or by subsequent contract.

Rule 2-105 Financial Payments

(A) A Representative shall not offer, promise or provide financial payments, support or consideration of any kind to an amateur athlete, his family members, athletic coach, director, school official or school with the intent to influence those persons or organizations into recommending that representative for employment by a professional athlete.
(B) The provisions contained in 2-105 (A) may not be waived in advance or by subsequent conduct.

Canon Three

A Representative shall maintain management responsibility for his firm.

Rule 3-101 A Representative Working with a Non-Representative

(A) A Representative shall not share fees with a non-Representative except:
  (1) A Representative may with the prior consent of the professional athlete he represents, retain the services of another professional or business entity on behalf of the athlete.
  (2) All charges in connection with such work shall be billed to the athlete directly or, at least, must be separately listed on the representatives' bill for services.

Rule 3-103 A Representative and the Player Contract

(A) A Representative shall not negotiate or agree to, on behalf of an athlete, any provision in a player contract which directly or indirectly violates or circumvents an operative collective bargaining agreement.
(B) ALL Representatives shall have a written contract with their clients which fully discloses all fees, duties and responsibilities. Such

contract shall fully disclose all matters in which the representative will receive a financial benefit.

(C) Any dispute arising out of a matter other than a dispute over fee shall be resolved by binding arbitration before an impartial arbitration panel set up for the particular sport in accordance with the rules of the American Arbitration Association.

(D) The supervision and administration of the binding arbitration shall be conducted by ARPA.

Canon Four

A Representative shall preserve the confidence of his client.

(A) A Representative shall not knowingly reveal information of any sort given to him by a client in the course of their professional relationship and which the client reasonably expects to be kept confidential.

(B) A Representative shall not use such confidential information to the direct or indirect disadvantage, harm, or damage of the client.

(C) A Representative shall not use such confidential information for his own advantage unless the client consents in advance after full disclosure by the representative.

Rule 4-102 Confidential Information Defined

(A) Confidential information refers to information gained in the course of the professional relationship between a representative and a professional athlete which the athlete has requested to be held confidential or which the representative knows or should know would be embarrassing or detrimental to the athlete if released.

Rule 4-103 Representative's Employees

(A) A Representative may reveal:
   (1) Confidential information with the written consent of the client after full disclosure by the representative,
   (2) Confidential information when required by law or directed by a tribunal,
   (3) Confidential information concerning illegal conduct past, present or future on the part of the athlete, except where such information is protected by the attorney/client privilege.

Canon Five

A Representative shall handle a Client matter competently.

(A) A Representative shall not handle a matter in the representation of a professional athlete if he knows or should know that he is not competent to handle such a matter.
(B) A Representative shall not handle a matter concerning a professional athlete without proper preparation and shall not neglect a matter entrusted to him by such a client.

Rule 5-102 A Representative Shall Actively Represent the Interests of His Client

(A) A Representative shall actively represent the interest of the professional athlete he represents.
(B) A Representative shall not knowingly make a public comment containing a false statement to his client's detriment.
(C) A Representative shall not knowingly make false statements concerning professional athletics of a professional athletic team or club.

Rule 5-103 A Representative Shall Avoid the Appearance of Impropriety

(A) A Representative shall preserve the identity of all client funds and of property which are given to him by or on behalf of a client.
    (1) A Representative shall maintain a separate bank account to retain client funds.
    (2) A Representative shall pay any interest earned on such an account to his client wherever practical.
(B) A Representative shall maintain complete records of client funds and property entrusted to the representative's care and shall render a record of such accounts to the client on a regular basis and upon request.
(C) A Representative shall conduct himself in his representation of professional athletes in such a manner as to avoid even the appearance of impropriety.

APPENDIX E

Addresses of Players and College Associations, Agents, and Sports Lawyers

Professional Players Associations

Canadian Football League Players Association
1686 Albert St.
Regina, Saskatchewan S4P-2S6
(306) 525–2158

Major Indoor Soccer League Players Association
1300 Connecticut Avenue, N.W.
Washington, D.C. 20036
(202) 463–2200

Major League Baseball Players Association
805 3rd Avenue
New York, NY 10022
(212) 826–0808

National Basketball Players Association
15 Columbus Circle
New York, NY 10023
(212) 541–7118

National Football League Players Association
1300 Connecticut Avenue, N.W., Suite 487
Washington, D.C. 20036
(202) 463–2200

National Hockey League Players Association
The Thomson Building
65 Queen Street, W., Suite 210
Toronto, Canada M5H-2M5
(416) 924–7800

Professional Golf Association Tour
Ponte Vedra Beach, FL 32082
(904) 285–3700

College Associations

National Association of Intercollegiate Athletics (NAIA)
National Headquarters
1221 Baltimore Avenue
Kansas City, MO 64105
(816) 842–5050
Executive Director: Jefferson D. Farris

National Collegiate Athletic Association (NCAA)
Nall Avenue at 63rd Street
P.O. Box 1906
Mission, KS 66201
(913) 384–3220
Executive Director: Richard Schultz

National Junior College Athletic Association (NJCAA)
P.O. Box 7305
Colorado Springs, CO 80933-7305
(303) 590–9788
Executive Director: George Killian

Association of Representatives of Professional Athletes (ARPA)
1000 Santa Monica Blvd., Suite 312
Los Angeles, CA 90067
  Mailing address:
  P.O. Box 90053
  World Way Postal Center
  Los Angeles, CA 90009
  (213) 553–5607

Association of Agents

Sports Lawyers Association
John Wendel, President
Box 5684
Lakeland, FL 33807
(813) 646–5091

Profiles of Top Agents and Management Groups (Sports Lawyers) Who Replied to the Survey

Steve Arnold (Pro Sports Inc.)
4386 Paradise Dr.
Tiburon, CA 94920
(415) 435–1211
Experience: 25 years
Fees: 5%

Andrew Brandt (ProServ, Inc.)
888 17th St., N.W.
Washington, D.C. 20006
(202) 466–1633
Experience: 3 years
Fees: Confidential

Ralph Cindrich (International Management Group)
5633 Steubenville Pike
Pittsburgh, PA 15244
(412) 787–1250
Experience: more than 10 years
Fees: 4% for negotiation; financial management is negotiable, depends on services needed

F. Harrison "Buzz" Green (Pro Sports Management)
11260 Chester Road
Cincinnati, OH 45246
(800) 543–6565
Experience: 15 years
Fees: *Football*

First round, $5,000 for negotiation, 2% financial
Second round, $5,000 negotiation, 3% financial
Third round, $5,000 negotiation, 4% financial
Fourth round, $5,000 negotiation, 5% financial

Fifth and sixth rounds, 7% full package
Seventh and eighth rounds, 8% full package
Ninth and tenth rounds, 9% full package
All others, 10% full package
Basketball
First round, $5,000 negotiation, 2% financial
Second round, $5,000 negotiation, 3% financial
All others, 10%
Existing professional athletes in any sport
$5,000 to negotiate any contract (even multiyear contracts); financial package for existing professional athletes varies

John Maloney (John Maloney, Inc.)
316 Diablo Road
Danville, CA 94526
(415) 838–9946
Experience: 16 years
Fees: First rounders, 1 1/2%
Second rounders, 2 1/2%
Third rounders, 3 1/2%
Fourth round and lower, 4%

Bob Woolf (Bob Woolf Associates, Inc.)
4575 Prudential Tower
Boston, MA 02199
(617) 437–1212
Experience: 25 years
Fees: Maximum of 5% on negotiation
Maximum of 5% on financial package

APPENDIX F

NCAA Career Counseling Panel Address List

University of Alabama, Tuscaloosa
P.O. Box 1435
Tuscaloosa, AL 35487-1435

Thomas L. Jones, *Chair*
Professor of Law
University of Alabama

Stanley Murphy
University Counsel's Office

Darryl Webb
College of Commerce and Business Administration

Gene Marsh
College of Commerce and Business Administration

George P. Taylor
School of Law

University of Arizona
Tucson, AZ 85721

Jack R. Cole, *Chair*
Dean, College of Pharmacy

Charles Smith
Professor, College of Law

	John E. Buehler Professor, Dept. of Economics
Arizona State University Tempe, AZ 85287	Alan Matheson, *Chair* Professor of Law Room 218
	Milton Schroeder Professor of Law
	Glenn Wilt Professor of Finance
Auburn University Auburn University, AL 36849-3501	Charles Edmonds III, *Chair* Professor, Dept. of Accnt. and Finance 305 Tichenor Hall
	Jane B. Moore Professor, HPER Room 2055/Memorial Coliseum
	Mark E. Meadows Professor, Dept. of Counselor Education 2010 Haley Center
	Hindman P. Wall Assoc. Director of Athletics Memorial Coliseum
Baptist College P.O. Box 10087 Baptist College at Charleston Charleston, SC 29411	David Rosin, *Chair* Professor of History
Baylor University Waco, Texas 76798	C.W. Thomas, *Chair* Professor of Accounting Hankamer School of Business
	Howard R. Dudgeon III University Treasurer CSB 419
	R. Michael Rogers Assistant Professor, School of Law CSB 364

Institution	Contacts
Boise State University Boise, ID 83725	Gene Bleymaier, *Chair* Director of Athletics Dick Bullington Vice President John Kaiser President Fred Norman Dir. of Morrison Center
Bowling Green State Univ. Bowling Green, OH 43403	Bob Holmes, *Chair* Associate Professor Legal Studies Steve Ludd Associate Professor, Pre-Law & Political Science Larry Kowalski Asst. Professor, Accounting and Mgmt. Info. System
Brigham Young University Provo, UT 84602	James W. Jenkins, *Chair* Associate Professor, School of Management 680 TNRB Chris Poulos Professor, Cont. Education 307 CEB James Backman Professor R. Reuben Clark Law School 430 JRCB Glen Tuckett Director of Athletics 106 SFH
Brooklyn College Bedford and H Avenues Brooklyn, NY 11210	Joe Margolis Director of Athletics

David Minars
Professor of Economics

Gregory A. Kuhlman
Dir. of Personnel Counseling

Ann Marie Mascolo
Special Assistant to the Pres. for Legal Affairs

Univ. of California, Irvine
Irvine, CA 92717

Thomas P. Parham, *Chair*
Director, Career Planning & Placement, SS I

Arthur Resnikoff
Counseling Psychologist
Counseling Center, SSI

Arnold Kaufman
Manager, Business & Contracts
313 Administration Bldg.

Robert Pomeroy
Asst. Dir. of Athletics
Crawford Hall

Univ. of California, Los Angeles
Los Angeles, CA 90024

Alfred E. Osborne, *Chair*
Associate Professor
Anderson Grad. School of Mgt.

William Klein
Professor
School of Law

Steven A. Lippman
Professor
Anderson Grad. School of Mgt.

Judith R. Holland
Sr. Assoc. Dir. of Athletics

California State Univ., Fresno
Fresno, CA 93740

Gerald Martin, *Chair*
Professor of Finance
School of Business and Admin. Sciences

Robert VanGalder
Professor, Phys. Ed. & Recreation

Walter Pierce
Asst. Dir. of Advising
Advising Center

Duke University
Durham, NC 27706

Eugene J. McDonald, *Chair*
Senior Vice President
Administration & Gen. Counsel

John C. Weistart
Professor of Law

A. Kenneth Pye
Professor of Law

Eastern Kentucky Univ.
Richmond, KY 40475

Russell Bogue, *Chair*
207 Begley Building

Jack Adams
Dept. of Physical Education

James Baechtold
Dept. of Recreation and Park Administration

Giles Black
Dept. of Police Admin.

University of Florida
Box J14 JHMHC
Gainesville, FL 32604

Kenneth F. Finger, *Chair*
Assoc. VP of Health Affairs

Dennis Calfee
Professor, School of Law
310 Holland Law Center

James E. Scott
Dean for Student Affairs
129 Tigert Hall

Florida A&M University
Tallahassee, FL 32307

Bishop Holifield, *Chair*
University Attorney

	Costa Kittles Associate Professor Division of Health, Phys. Ed. and Recreation
	Leo Sams Vice Pres. for Univ. Relations
Florida State University Tallahassee, FL 32306	Charles Ehrhardt, *Chair* Professor, College of Law
	James P. Jones Professor, Dept. of History
	Marc G. Gertz Professor, School of Criminology
Furman University Greenville, SC 29613	Francis W. Bonner, *Chair* Professor of English
	R. Wayne Weaver Vice Pres., Business Affairs
	Schaefer B. Kendrick Professor of Economics
Georgia Inst. of Tech. Atlanta, GA 30332	Dick Fuller, *Chair* Vice President, Finance
	Leroy Emkin Professor, Civil Engineering
	William Sangster Dean, College of Engineering
University of Georgia Athens, GA 30602	Timothy W. Floyd, *Chair* Professor, School of Law
	Wayne W. Antenen Professor, Counselor Educ.
	Asa T. Boynton Director, Office of Public Safety

Grambling State Univ. P.O. Box 68 Grambling, LA 71245	E. M. Jones, *Chair* Asst. Prof., Dept. of English Mrs. Elizabeth Britton Insurance Clerk Gene Blakley Dir. of Student Financial Aid
University of Hawaii 2530 Dole Street Honolulu, HI 96822	Joseph Choy, *Chair* Dean, College of Cont. Educ. Sakamaki Hall C401 Richard Miller Dean, School of Law David Bess Dean, College of Bus. Admin. Bus. Admin. Bldg. C204
University of Houston 4800 Calhoun Road Houston, TX 77004	Richard Alderman Professor of Law Jeffrey Sammons Assistant Professor of History College of Humanities & Fine Arts Samuel Smith Professor of Marketing College of Business Admin.
Univ. of Illinois, Urbana-Champaign	John E. Nowak, *Chair* Professor, College of Law 113 Law Building 504 E. Pennsylvania Avenue Champaign, IL 61820 James A. Gentry Professor, Dept. of Finance 144 Commerce West 1206 S. 6th Street Champaign, IL 61820

Philip E. Fess
Professor, Dept. of Accntg.
209 Commerce West
1206 S. 6th Street
Champaign, IL 61820

Indiana Univ.,
Bloomington
Bloomington, IN 47405

Albert J. Velasquez, *Chair*
Office of the Univ. Counsel
Bryan Hall 304

Mr. John A. Scanlon
School of Law

Samuel Frumer
School of Business

Iowa State University
Ames, IA 50011

Larry Curtis, *Chair*
Adjunct Asst. Prof. Management
347 Carver Hall

Wilfred Dellva
Asst. Professor, Finance

Vern Hawkins
Asst. Dir., Admissions & Records

Jackson State
University
Jackson, MS 39217

John Hurley, *Chair*
Department of Economics

Charles Henry Holmes
Assoc. Prof. of Political Science

Eunice T. Smith
Dept. of Bus. Educ. & Administrative
Services

James Madison
University
Harrisonburg, VA 22807

Eileen S. Nelson, *Chair*
Assoc. Professor, Psychology

Harold J. McGee
VP of Administrative Affairs

Thomas A. Nardi
Dir., Career Planning & Placement

University of Kentucky
Lexington, KY 40506-0032

Jack Blanton, *Chair*
Vice Chancellor for Admin.
110 Administration Bldg.

C. W. Ellinger
Professor, College of Dentistry
D540 Chandler Medical Center

William James
Director of Law Library
Room 124, Law Library

La Salle University
Philadelphia, PA 19141

Peter J. Filicetti
Asst. Prof. of Psychology

Laura A. Otten
Asst. Prof. of Sociology

Broth. Arthur J. Bangs, F.S.C.
Asst. Professor of Education

University of Louisville
Louisville, KY 40292

Bruce H. Kemelgor, *Chair*
Dept. of Mgt., School of Bus.

William R. Flatt
Assoc. VP for Administration

Tara S. Singer
Athletic Academic Counselor

Edwin P. Render
Professor of Law

Jack Tennant
Athletic Associates, Inc.

Univ. of Maine, Orono
Orono, ME 04469

Albert F. Hackett, *Chair*
Assoc. Director of Admissions
Chadbourne Hall

Robert A. Strong
Assistant Professor
28C South Stevens Hall

	Walter H. Abbott Associate Professor 103 Lengyel Gymnasium
Univ. of Miami Coral Gables, FL 33124	Robert Waters, *Chair* School of Law Room 462, Law Library
	Irwin Stotzky School of Law Room 461, Law Library
	William McElrath Director, School of Business Room 212, Jenkings Bldg.
Univ. of Minnesota, Twin Cities Minneapolis, MN 55455	John Matheson, *Chair* Professor, School of Law 285 Law Center
	Ed Joyce Professor, School of Mgmt.
	Stephen Befort Professor, School of Law
Univ. of Mississippi University, MS 38677	Robert Khayat, *Chair* Vice Chancellor, Univ. Affairs
	Gordon Beasley Vice Chanc., Student Affairs
	Mary Ann Connell Special Asst. to Chancellor
Mississippi College Clinton, MS 39058	James Burnside, *Chair* Mississippi College Box 4245
	Anne Meydrech Mississippi College Box 4045

	Charles E. Martin Mississippi College Box 4086
Mississippi State Univ. Mississippi State, MS 39762	S. Jones, *Chair* Professor of Marketing
	William L. Ware Mississippi State Univ.
	Walter Newsome Assoc. Professor, Mgmt. Drawer MG
Univ. of Missouri, Columbia Columbia, MO 65211	Loren Nikolai, *Chair* Professor, Accounting 312 Middlebush
	George Wallach Professor of Law 230 Tate Hall
	Hardeep Bhullar Assoc. Prof., Recreation & Parks Admin. 625 Clark Hall
University of Montana Missoula, MT 59812	Jack Morton Prof. of Business Law
	W. Arthur Graham Assoc. Prof. of Business Law
	Rudyard Goode Professor of Finance School of Bus. Admin.
Univ. of Nebraska, Lincoln Lincoln, NE 68588-0419	James O'Hanlon Richard Wood
	Richard Metcalf

Univ. of New Mexico
Albuquerque, NM 87131

Gary Ness, *Chair*
Assoc. Prof. HPER Dept.
Johnson Gym 210-B

Thomas Brennan
Assoc. Director of Athletics

Pat McNamara
Sociology Department

Alfred Mathewson
Asst. Prof., School of Law

Nicholls State Univ.
Thibodaux, LA 70310

Jerry Hood, *Chair*
Assoc. Prof., Econ. & Finance

Jerry Dalrymple
Instructor, Mgmt. & Marketing

John Simmons
Asst. Prof., Accounting

Univ. of North Carolina,
Chapel Hill
Chapel Hill, NC 27514

Dean Smith, *Chair*
Head Basketball Coach
P.O. Box 2126

Jack Evans
Dean, School of Bus. Admin.
Carroll Hall 012A

Ken Brown
Dean, Law School
Van Hecke-Wettach Bldg. 064A

Elson Floyd
Assistant Dean
Office of Vice Chanc. of Student Affairs
207 Steele Bldg. 05A

Univ. of North Carolina,
Charlotte
Charlotte, NC 28223

Thomas C. Turner, *Chair*
Department of Accounting

Louis A. Trosch
Assoc. Prof. of Bus. Admin

R. B. Simono
Director, Counseling Center

North Carolina State Univ.
Raleigh, NC 27695-7001

Carl J. Messere
Economics & Business Dept.

Becky R. Frency
University Counsel
Box 7001

James T. Valvano
Director of Athletics
Box 8501

Norfolk State Univ.
2401 Corprew Avenue
Norfolk, VA 23504

Rudolph Smith, *Chair*
Atty. and Asst. VP of Finance & Business

Henrietta Dabney
Asst. Dean, School of General/Cont. Education

Joseph Scott
Graduate Student

North Texas State Univ.
Denton, TX 76203

J. R. Lott, *Chair*
Professor of Biology

William Neu
Pharmacist
2100 Southridge Drive

James L. McDonald
Assoc. Prof. of Finance
P.O. Box 13677

University of Notre Dame
Notre Dame, IN 46556

Fernand Dutile, *Chair*
Law School

Professor Kenneth Milani

Rev. William Beauchamp

Old Dominion University H & PE Building Norfolk, VA 23508	Mark Newman, *Chair* Head Baseball Coach Melvin Williams Graduate Advisor/Instructor Room 134 Charles Sweet Counsel to University Room 214-B New Administration Bldg.
University of Oklahoma Norman, OK 73019	Stanley Ward, *Chair* Chief Legal Counsel Anthony Bluitt Assoc. Professor of Law Paul Wilson Dir., Recreational Services
Oklahoma State Univ. 107 Whitehurst Stillwater, OK 74078	Joe W. Fosler, *Chair* Exec. Asst. to President Howard Shipp Coordinator of Minority Programs and Services 0315 Student Union William G. Simpson Prof. & Head, Dept. of Finance 201 College of Bus. Admin.
Pennsylvania State Univ. University Park, PA 16802	Kenneth Lusht, *Chair* Professor, Bus. Admin. 409L Bus. Administration Building Randall J. Woolridge Assoc. Professor of Finance 609 Business Administration Building Jack Williams Professor, Admin. of Justice 314 Sields Building

Univ. of Pennsylvania
Philadelphia, PA 19104-6303

Paul Zing, *Chair*
Asst. to President
100 College Hall

Univ. of Pittsburgh
3200 Cathedral of Learning
Pittsburgh, PA 15260

Lewis M. Popper, *Chair*
University Counsel

John O. Bolvin
Dean of College of General Studies
416 Cathedral of Learning

William J. Brown
Professor, School of Law
302 Law Building

University of Richmond
Richmond, VA 23173

Robert E. Shepherd, Jr., *Chair*
T. C. Williams School of Law

Richard J. Dunsing
Dir. of Institute of Bus. & Comm. Devel.

Harold W. Babb
Associate Professor
Department of Marketing

John H. Earl, Jr.
Assistant Professor
Department of Finance

Rutgers University,
New Brunswick
New Brunswick, NJ 08903

Malcolm McLaren, *Chair*
Faculty Athletics Rep.
College of Engineering

Lee D. Schneider
Associate Dean

David R. Scott
University Counsel

San Diego State Univ.
San Diego, CA 92182

Daniel B. Nowak, *Chair*
V. Pres., Student Affairs

David Nesvig
Counselor, Counseling Services
and Placement

Allan R. Bailey
Dir., Admin. & Bus. Services

Joseph Vasquez
Director, Student Outreach Services

Ernst Griffin
Professor of Geography

Penny Wright
Dean, School of Bus. Admin.

Patricia Sandback
Professor, Physical Educ.

George Hutchinson
Professor of Management

Univ. of San Francisco
Ignatian Heights
San Francisco, CA
94117-1080

Mr. Eamonn Barrett, *Chair*
School of Business

Rev. Robert A. Sunderland
Director of Athletics

Mr. David Scalise
School of Business

Univ. of South Alabama
Mobile, AL 36688

Jeral R. Williams, *Chair*
Vice Pres. for Academic Affairs

J. Ronnie Davis
Dean of College of Business and
Mgmt. Services

Joe Gottfried
Director of Athletics

Normal Hill
President
Gulf Coast Safety Products

Univ. of South Carolina
Columbia, SC 29208

David Shipley, *Chair*
School of Law

	Timothy Koch College of Business
	Rodney Roenfeldt College of Business
	Harold A. White Department of Athletics
Univ. of South Florida Tampa, FL 33620	Dan Wolbolt, *Chair* Vice President, Office of Student Affairs ADM 151
	Troy Collier Assistant to Vice President Office of Student Affairs ADM 151
	Carla Jimenez Legal Affairs ADM 250
Southern University, Baton Rouge Baton Rouge, LA 70813	Clarence Cunningham, *Chair* Vice Chancellor of Admin.
	Clyde Tidwell Law School Professor
	Thelma Bradford College of English
Stanford University Stanford, CA 94305	William Gould, *Chair* Professor of Law
	Tom Heller Professor of Law
	Roger Noll Professor of Economics
Syracuse University Syracuse, NY 13210	Ronald R. Cavanagh, *Chair* Assoc. Dean, Arts & Sciences 329 Hall of Languages

	Travis H. Lewin Professor, College of Law
Temple University Philadelphia, PA 19122	Mary Ellen Krober, *Chair* Assoc. University Counsel
	John G. Spiese Office of Student Affairs
	Michael Jackson College of HPERD
Texas A&I University Kingsville, TX 78383	Randy Hughes, *Chair* Director, Intramurals
	Jim Norwine Professor Geosciences
	Arturo Pecos Financial Aid Officer
Univ. of Texas, Arlington Arlington, TX 76019	Eugene Anderson, *Chair* Professor & Chairman Dept. of Physical Educ.
	John S. Robottom Asst. to the Dean College of Engineering
	Terry Witt Associate Professor Dept. of Accounting
Univ. of Texas, Austin Austin, TX 78712	John M. Quinn, *Chair* Asst. Dean, School of Comm.
	Robert E. Witt Dean, School of Bus. Admin.
	John T. Ratliff, Jr. Professor, School of Law
Trinity College Hartford, CT 06106	Gerald J. Hansen, Jr. Director, Alumni & College Relations

	Drew Hyland Professor of Philosophy
Tulane University New Orleans, LA 70015	Gary Roberts, *Chair* Professor, School of Law Tulane Law School
	Ronald Mason University Attorney
	Thomas Andre Professor, School of Law
University of Utah Salt Lake City, UT 84112	Don Zillman, *Chair* Professor, College of Law
	Kaye Coleman Assoc. Director, Equal Opor. 411 Park Building
	Ron Coleman Asst. Professor, Dept. of History
	Larry Gerlach Professor, Dept. of History
University of Virginia Charlottesville, VA 22901	Alex M. Johnson, Jr., *Chair* Asst. Professor, School of Law North Grounds
	William G. Shenkir Dean, McIntire School of Commerce 209 Monroe Hall
	Robert J. Rotella Assoc. Professor of Health School of Education 405 Emmet Street
VA Polytechnic Institute Blacksburg, VA 24061	James Robertson, *Chair* Professor of History
	Jane B. Bulgin General Counsel

	Raymond D. Smoot, Jr. Assoc. Vice Pres. & Treasurer
Wake Forest University Winston-Salem, NC 27109	Don Castleman, *Chair* School of Law P.O. Box 7206
	Edward Felton, Jr. School of Management P.O. Box 7659
	John Sawyer Department of Mathematics P.O. Box 7401
University of Washington Seattle, WA 98195	Steve Goldblatt, *Chair* Dept. of Bldg. Construction 208 Gould JO-24
	John Keating Professor, School of Psych. 217 Guthrie NI-25
	Arval Morris Professor, School of Law 1100 NE Campus Pkwy JB-20
	Thaddeus Spratlen Professor, School of Bus. 210 Mackenzie DJ-10
West Virginia University Morgantown, WV 26507	Fred Schauss Director of Athletics
	Frank Cleckley Professor, Law School
	Jeffrey C. Dyer Accounting and Finance
	Paul L. Selby Professor, Law School

University of Wisconsin,
Stevens Point
Stevens Point, WI 54481

Virgil Thiesfeld, *Chair*
Chairman, Biology Dept.

Myrvin Christopherson
Chrmn. Comm. Department
Comm. Arts Center

Leonard Gibb
Director of Development

William Johnson
Asst. Dean, College of Letters and Sciences
Collins Classroom

APPENDIX G

Sample of the Proper Approach to a First-Round NFL Contract

Introduction

Pro Sports Management is committed to only one objective in advising its clients on financial matters: *LIFETIME FINANCIAL INDEPENDENCE.* It should be possible, given the size of a first-round contract and endorsement opportunities, to achieve this goal. A well-conceived financial plan is critical to success and must take into account a number of important factors:

1. The professional athlete will make a great deal of money in a very short period of time.
2. The athlete's high risk of injury may abruptly end or disrupt his career.
3. Major sports figures are exposed to intense public scrutiny in their personal conduct, including their financial affairs.

A financial plan is very much like a game plan. It attempts to maximize strengths and minimize weaknesses. It takes into account contingencies so that surprises don't upset the entire plan. Certain strategies are used to "set up" other strategies. The plan is divided into sections that are implemented depending upon "which quarter the game is in." Most importantly, the financial plan, like the game plan, fixes some firm objectives and details how those objectives will be attained.

Purpose

The purpose of this proposal is threefold:

1. To describe Pro Sports Management's financial planning philosophy,
2. To detail how a hypothetical first-round contract might be invested,
3. To illustrate, using sophisticated computer projections, the impact of invested dollars on net worth, cash flow, and taxes.

Financial Planning Philosophy

The foundation of Pro Sports Management's financial planning philosophy rests on four primary tenants:

1. A financial plan is unique to an individual and must take into account special circumstance, priorities, and desires of that particular athlete.
2. The initial four-year contract must emphasize secure investments that offer flexibility, liquidity, and income deferral.
3. Second and third contracts provide the opportunity for diversification into less liquid, more speculative investments. Preparation for a post-NFL career is primary.
4. Tax avoidance is important but should not be stressed at the sacrifice of long-range goals. Income deferral is a preferred tax avoidance technique to "tax shelters."

Hypothetical Four-Year Contract and Endorsements

1. Cash signing bonus of $500,000
2. Interest-free demand loan of $500,000
3. 1990–91 base salary of $600,000 increasing by $75,000 in each contract year
4. Deferred compensation in the form of a *guaranteed* monthly income of $16,300 beginning September of 1998 continuing for 48 months
5. Endorsement income of $100,000 in 1990 and $250,000 in each of the following years

Strategies

1. Establish a personal services corporation for endorsement income. A defined benefit pension plan can be established inside the corporation

that would allow deductible contributions of $100,000 per year for 10 years. The corporation can retain $150,000 in earnings that would create additional tax savings.

2. The proceeds from the interest-free loan should be used to purchase a personal residence.
3. Establish a budget that permits expenses of $80,000 in 1990, increasing by $10,000 each year through 1994. An additional $70,000 can be made available for spending in 1990 from the cash signing bonus.
4. 1990 cash surplus (approximately $370,000) should be placed in a tax-free money fund earning four percent after tax. This fund will serve as a base of liquidity and cash reserve. Late in the first contract (perhaps 1992) the fund will be reduced in size as other liquid assets have accumulated.
5. Beginning in 1991, invest $150,000 in a single premium deferred annuity. At present, a nine percent return guaranteed for ten years is available on a tax-deferred basis. Another $150,000 should be invested in 1992 and again in 1993. This money will accumulate as a possible income source beginning in 2000.
6. The remaining cash surplus available in 1991 through 1994 should be split between intermediate term municipal bonds and growth-oriented common stocks. By 1994 the combined stock and bond portfolio should be worth in excess of $830,000.
7. While an IRA contribution of $2,000 is relatively insignificant, tax deductions must be taken wherever possible.

APPENDIX H

Questionnaire

Questions to Ask When Hiring an Agent	Agent Name ______	Agent Name ______	Agent Name ______	Agent Name ______
A. Qualifications of negotiator or negotiating team				
1. What expertise does he have in general contract negotiations?				
2. What experience does he have in negotiating for athletes?				
3. What type of expertise does he have in contract law in general?				

Questions to Ask When Hiring an Agent	Agent Name ______	Agent Name ______	Agent Name ______	Agent Name ______
4. Is he registered with the NCAA?				
5. Is he registered with the NFL Players Assn.?				
6. Is the certification permanent or annual?				
7. How long has he been in business?				
8. Have there been any complaints to the players union about this agent?				
9. Has the agent provided educational credentials?				
10. Has agent provided references?				
B. Qualifications of the money management team				
1. Is the representative a C.F.A. (Chartered Financial Analyst—the highest rating in the field)?				

Questions to Ask When Hiring an Agent	Agent Name ______	Agent Name ______	Agent Name ______	Agent Name ______
2. Is agent a CFP (a certified financial planner—an easy license used primarily by insurance salesmen)?				
3. Does he have special expertise:				
in banking?				
in securities?				
in real estate?				
4. Is he a "hands-on" manager (whereas he handles your money)?				
5. Is he "hands-off" (whereas you control your money)?				
6. Is a financial plan developed?				
7. What does the financial plan cost you?				
8. How is the financial plan developed?				

Questions to Ask When Hiring an Agent	Agent Name ______	Agent Name ______	Agent Name ______	Agent Name ______
9. Does agent ever take commissions or kickbacks on financial dealings he arranges with you, such as:				
insurance sales?				
limited partnerships?				
sale of stocks or bonds?				
10. Does he sell any kind of insurance?				
11. Will he ever ask for a power of attorney to make your investments?				
C. The qualifications of the tax-planning person				
1. Is he a certified public accountant (CPA)?				
2. What is the strength of his company?				
3. What experience has he had with the special tax problems of athletes?				

Questions to Ask When Hiring an Agent	Agent Name ______	Agent Name ______	Agent Name ______	Agent Name ______
D. Strength analysis before pro camp				
1. Does agent do film analysis to discover your strengths and weaknesses so that you can work to improve yourself before the pro camp?				
2. Who does the film analysis?				
3. What are his qualifications?				
4. What sort of report do they develop?				
5. What are the qualifications of the person making the recommendations?				
6. How does the agent get you into camp?				
7. What are his contacts?				

Questions to Ask When Hiring an Agent	**Agent Name** ______	**Agent Name** ______	**Agent Name** ______	**Agent Name** ______
E. Available Experts				
1. What types of experts are available to you through the agent?				
2. Is there a charge for these services?				
F. Evaluation of the honesty of agent				
1. Did the agent offer you money before your eligibility was completed? (*This is unethical and illegal under the criminal code.*)				
2. Did he offer you money (such as a loan) to sign? (*This is unethical and a breach of contract law under the civil codes.*)				
3. Have any complaints ever been lodged against him? (*Check with the player associations to determine.*)				

Questions to Ask When Hiring an Agent	Agent Name ______	Agent Name ______	Agent Name ______	Agent Name ______
4. If he is going to handle any money, is he bonded?				
G. Contract Structure				
1. How is the contract structured?				
2. What provisions are inserted to protect you?				
H. Education interest				
1. Does he ask you to drop out of school?				
2. Is he interested in helping you get your degree?				
I. Financial problems				
1. If you need money early, how is it handled?				
2. If you want insurance, what does he do?				
3. If you want a car, how does he help you?				

Questions to Ask When Hiring an Agent	Agent Name ______	Agent Name ______	Agent Name ______	Agent Name ______
4. Does agent provide any special banking services?				
5. What do the special banking services cost?				
J. Agent's fees				
1. What money must agent pay for your well-being?				
2. What are agent's fees?				
3. Do agent fees cover:				
negotiating?				
daily accounting?				
doing all taxes?				
private banking?				
financial planning?				
investment recommendations?				
4. Does agent charge you expenses for:				

Questions to Ask When Hiring an Agent	Agent Name ______	Agent Name ______	Agent Name ______	Agent Name ______
phone?				
travel?				
K. Endorsements				
1. What are the possibilities of endorsements?				
2. What would you need to do to get endorsement money?				
3. What record does agent have in getting endorsements for his players?				
4. What is agent's program for making you marketable?				
L. Retirement				
1. Does agent have a retirement plan available?				
2. How is the retirement plan structured?				

Questions to Ask When Hiring an Agent	Agent Name ______	Agent Name ______	Agent Name ______	Agent Name ______
M. Agent's: strengths				
1. Does agent emphasize that he is better because he is small or local?				
2. Does he have regional representatives so that wherever you play you will have a personal contact?				
3. Is he available through an (800) line at no cost to you?				
4. Does he have special expertise in athletics?				
5. Does he have strong contacts with both the NFL and Canadian leagues?				
N. Agent's special services				
1. Does he provide for:				
psychologist?				
marriage counselor?				

Questions to Ask When Hiring an Agent	Agent Name ______	Agent Name ______	Agent Name ______	Agent Name ______
weight training and conditioning specialists?				
O. Summary and special considerations				
1. Is the agent one who is interested in the long-term goals of the athlete?				
2. What are agent's fees?				
3. What do agent's fees cover?				
4. Are the fees paid:				
up front?				
as earned?				
5. Are all of the agent's expenses covered in the fees?				
6. Are the fees billed:				
as a percentage of income?				
as a flat fee?				

Questions to Ask When Hiring an Agent	Agent Name ______	Agent Name ______	Agent Name ______	Agent Name ______
as an hourly fee?				
7. Overall, how do you rate agent's qualifications, services, and concern?				